FOOD
CAN DAMAGE
YOUR HEALTH

ROSTERS LTD

FOOD
CAN DAMAGE
YOUR HEALTH

Jane Bowden and
Rosemary Burr

ROSTERS LTD

Published by ROSTERS LTD
60 Welbeck Street, London W1

© Bowden and Burr 1989
ISBN 0-948032-08-1

Designed and published by ROSTERS
Typeset by Gwynne Printers, Hurstpierpoint, Sussex
Printed and bound in Great Britain by Cox & Wyman Ltd, Reading

First edition 1989

About the authors

Jane Bowden was born in Newcastle-on-Tyne and as the daughter of a Royal Air Force Officer spent much of her childhood living overseas. She started her career nursing and worked in a refugee camp in Korangi, just outside Karachi in West Pakistan. That was followed by a period working in military hospitals in West Germany. Her experience in the health field includes lecturing to industry as a consultant on developing resources and stress management, teaching health management to over 60 groups, writing on such topics as anorexia for *The Gymnast*, author of *Maintaining Your Fitness and Health* and a consultant author of Shirley Cooper's *Good Health Guide*. She also broadcasts on the topic of health and holistic medicine, and consumer matters.

Rosemary Burr was born in London and studied Politics, Philosophy and Economics at Oxford University. She then joined the Financial Times Group and worked there for seven years. While there she investigated the downfall of the Norton Warburg Group, Doxfords, and rogue liquidators. In 1985 she wrote and published her bestselling guide to the stock market, *The Share Book*, and since then has written two books a year on various money and business matters. She also broadcasts regularly on consumer affairs for both local and national radio.

Contents

INTRODUCTION

Is our food safe to eat? A year ago that would have seemed a daft question raised perhaps by a few extreme health cranks who believed that processed food equalled bad food. Sadly today the question is all too relevant and in need of an urgent, unequivocal answer.

Almost every day we hear on the radio and television about a new food scare. First it was eggs, then chickens, then cheese and the week before Easter doubts were raised about chocolate cream eggs. We were also told about unwelcome pesticides lurking unseen and unsuspected in our potatoes, bran cereal and lettuces.

The first aim of this book was therefore simply to put together the available information on the state of British food and water. This turned out to be a Herculean task in itself. We then tried to assess these facts as objectively as possible by talking to as many people as possible. We talked to more than 200 people, each of whom added a new perspective to the debate. We discussed the state of our food and water with scientists, with doctors, with food producers, with manufacturers, with retailers, with lobbyists such as the Friends of the Earth and with Government departments. The reaction was mixed. Some people went out of their way to be helpful and to supply us with data, in other quarters we were met with stony silence. Finally when we asked certain government officials for data we were told this was not publicly available.

Despite the difficulties in getting the information on our food and water we have been able to build up a comprehensive picture which we believe will help the consumer shop more wisely. We have also put together tips from the experts to help you protect yourself from what are undoubtedly the potential hazards lurking invisibly in some of our basic food stuffs as well as in some of the pre-packaged and processed products we eat and drink.

The research for this book has also helped us to draw up a charter for a change; a list of new rules and regulations required to help restore consumer's confidence in British food and water. There is a desperate need for the publication of more information so that independent experts outside government departments can monitor more effectively the true state of our food and drink. We have also been looking to the future and have assessed the impact of '1992 and all that' when we may well be flooded by imports from our partners in the European Community.

While many of the facts we have uncovered make gloomy reading, we do not feel there is a case for despair. The future state of our food and drink is in our own hands. There is a great deal of room for improvement, for example, ways we can tighten up on hygiene and safety requirements. Added to that although the scientists cannot always tell us just what is a safe level of say pesticide residue in our food their powers of detection and analysis are improving by leaps and bounds. It is up to the rest of us to make certain these new advances are put to work to ensure a higher quality of food and water in the 1990's.

CHAPTER ONE:
WHAT'S BUGGING US?

Our guess is that most people reading this book have either suffered a bout of mild food poisoning in the last eighteen months – or that they know a friend who has. We use the word 'guess' deliberately. The truth is we simply do not know just how many people are affected by food poisoning. The reason for this sorry situation is two-fold. First, the government statistics on food poisoning are collated by the Communicable Disease Surveillance Centre and published in confidential weekly reports which are despatched to environmental health officers around the country. The statistics are not for publication until the government of the day decides we can all be told. Second, everyone concerned, from doctors through to microbiologists, and even the government have gone on record as saying that the statistics woefully underestimate the true nature of the problem. Quite simply most people with food poisoning don't bother to visit their doctor and if they do see one then the doctor is likely to treat their symptoms, not offer to investigate the cause unless and until the disease fails to respond.

What the figures show

So everyone agrees that these 'secret' statistics on food

poisoning grossly underplay the problem we are facing. The key question becomes then by how much? We have talked to a number of scientists and microbiologists on this question. The consensus is that reports of minor food poisoning outbreaks should be multiplied by a figure of up to 100 to give a true representation. Please keep this in mind when reading the following statistics which we obtained from the Department of Health and Social Security press office in early March:

DHSS FIGURES ON FOOD POISONING

Food bug	No. cases	Deaths (if known)	Year
Salmonella (total)	24,123	na	1988
Salmonella (eggs)	1,600	na	1988
Listeriosis	291	61*	1988
Campylobacter	20,861	na	1984
Campylobacter	25,900	na	1987

*This figure represents patients who died and who had listeriosis – some were suffering from other diseases such as AIDS and so this figure does not represent an accurate picture of those who died *due* to listeriosis.

These figures only provide a small part of the total picture since obviously we need to get a historical perspective and to narrow down the type of salmonella bacteria more closely. However, they do highlight the following points:

- the most common source of illness which *may* be related to food is not salmonella but campylobacter. The Department of Health and Social Services

14

emphasised that only a small percentage of these cases have been traced to food, that campylobacter was widespread in the environment, present in some raw chicken carcases and there was a tendency to be single cases of infection – not outbreaks where several people are infected.

- the number of people suffering from campylobacter rose by nearly a quarter between 1984 and 1987.

- the number of cases traced to eggs infected with salmonella was one in every fifteen.

- listeriosis is still a relatively minor problem – but is a serious health threat since it can be a contributory factor in the death of patients *already* suffering from other diseases.

Historical perspective

As we have noted, the figures for salmonella and listeriosis represent a single year. True they may be a vast under-representation, but are they so much worse than previous years? Sadly, the answer is 'yes'. Twenty years ago in 1969 the total number of recorded cases of bacterial food poisoning in England and Wales was officially placed at 8,209; eight years ago in 1981 this figure was 10,665 and five years ago in 1984 it stood at 15,312. From the raw data we have been provided for last year we can estimate a figure in the region of 50,000.

An epidemic

To underline the fact that we are indeed facing a

worsening trend we have talked to both environmental health officers, doctors and scientists around the country. In the first two months of 1988 roughly 4,000 cases of salmonella poisoning were reported but over the same period of 1989 the figure had surged to over 6,000. That is a 50% rise and a large enough increase in the number of cases to justify the label 'epidemic'. What is worse, they say that the weekly figures for this year show a continued deterioration of the situation. Of course, for the exact figures we will have to wait until the government deigns to tell us.

At current rates we could expect 36,000 notified cases in 1989 which, given the level of under-reporting, could turn out to represent 3.6 million actual cases of food poisoning by salmonella alone. If we assume optimistically that cases related to campylobacter do not increase and that they too are under-reported by a factor of 100 we will be looking at just over 6 million cases of food poisoning in the UK for 1989. That's roughly one in ten of the population who will suffer.

Enter the egg

Is the poor old egg to blame for the rise in salmonella poisoning? The official statistics from the Department of Health and Social Security seem to suggest otherwise. Just one in every fifteen cases last year was traced to eggs which were 'raw' and when it first warned the public in a press release on August 26, 1988 the Department of Health said 'in terms of UK consumption of around 30 million eggs a day, the incidence of *known* (our italics) infection is very small.'

In our view the crucial word here is 'known'. It must be stressed that tracing the source of food poisoning is often difficult and pinning the blame on the actual culprit even harder. Salmonella and listeria are common in our environment. Indeed probably one in every ten readers of this book is, unknown to them, a carrier of salmonella, and between one and five in every 100 may be a carrier of listeria. We do not and cannot in normal circumstances outside an intensive care wing of a hospital or a space ship eat 'sterile' food. Bacteria of all sorts, both harmful and beneficial, are present in us, in the environment, and in our food.

So when considering the evidence as to the possible 'cause' of this growing hazard from salmonella we need to remember that the scientists are doing their best to produce likely scenarios which fit the existing facts and hence 'explain' matters in a way the rest of us regard as satisfactory. Since the facts are difficult to ascertain – for example, you cannot trace an egg back to its producer in this country and you cannot test a representative sample of eggs – it is perhaps not surprising that the scientific community is divided about the source of this growing problem.

● Pointing the finger at eggs

The chief proponent of the view that eggs are the culprit is the professor for clinical microbiology at the university of Leeds, Richard Lacey, incidentally dubbed 'Mr Listeria' by one newspaper recently. He has analysed the statistics for salmonella up to the end of 1988 and concludes that: the growth in salmonella outbreaks is due to a strain called 'salmonella enteritidis' and in particular a strain generally known as 'enteritidis phage type 4'. This he argues has been shown to be associated in *most cases* (our italics) with foods containing egg ingredients. He also points to evidence of *one* (our italics) flock where this type 4 strain was found in 26% of the birds and in some of the eggs which they laid.

He concludes therefore that 'the *only* (his italics) plausible explanation for the dramatic rise in salmonella enteritidis food poisoning' is infected flocks laying infected eggs.

● Pointing the finger at the chicken

The scientists on this side of the argument say, just because we have a new strain does not mean that we have a new source of infection. In other words, as the poor old chicken has been shown to harbour the new strain in some cases we don't need to complicate matters by assuming we are infected by eggs, rather than by the chicken itself. Indeed Professor Lacey says: 'it is certainly possible that *some* (our italics) of the food poisoning from salmonella enteritidis could be from chicken meat, but there would *appear* (our italics) to be no reason for such an increase.' Indeed, the agriculture committee's first report, Salmonella In Eggs, published on February 28, 1989 admitted there was a 'scarcity of positive evidence'. However, that report concluded there was 'weighty circumstantial evidence', which was sufficient to point the finger at eggs.

So how safe is an egg?

We do not know how many flocks are carrying salmonella, let along how many are infected with the new strain type 4. Even if we knew how many flocks were infected and how many eggs they produced we could not say how many of those eggs would themselves be infected nor the degree of that infection.

We leave the reader to weigh up the evidence and to ponder the answer to the above question supplied by the agriculture committee's first report:

'The risk to individual consumers cannot be quantified exactly, but given that the likelihood of an egg being infected with salmonella is very small, and the likelihood of the infection not being destroyed by cooking is even smaller, normally healthy people should feel no cause for concern. Those who consume uncooked eggs or uncooked egg dishes should be aware that these carry a slight risk. Care should be taken to cook eggs thoroughly for vulnerable groups, in line with the Chief Medical Officer's advice'.

The Chief Medical Officer's advice published in a press release on August 26, 1988 was that people 'already weakened by disease, the very young or the very old' should 'avoid eating raw eggs or uncooked foods made from them, such as home-made mayonnaise, home made mousses and home-made ice cream, as well as raw eggs mixed into drinks. Caterers are being advised to use pasteurised egg for uncooked dishes.'

Just what does it take to kill off this new super strain salmonella enteritidis type 4? Here again the scientists disagree. Notably Professor Lacey who argues that type 4 may be more heat resistant than many others believe, in which case the egg needs to be cooked longer than is the case with our normal method of preparing omelettes, scrambled eggs and souffles.

Listeria hysteria

Listeria is a bacteria which is found all around us. If listeria is fairly common why do some people get a disease from it which can be fatal? So far the scientists have not come up with the answers. They do not know enough about the bacteria to know how we become infected nor whether food is implicated.

As Dr. J. Verner Wheelock, head of the independent Food Policy Research Unit, states: 'it is not in the least surprising that listeria should be found in a variety of foods . . . furthermore it is extremely difficult to determine whether its presence constitutes a serious hazard since we do not know how and why an infection does occur.' Similarly Dr. Spence Galbraith, director of the Communicable Disease Centre, has stated that 'Listeriosis remained uncommon and its association with food has yet to be defined.'

There is evidence from the USA, Canada and Switzerland that large outbreaks of listeriosis could be linked back to food highly contaminated with listeria. The interesting thing is that in this country most cases of listeria reported are isolated cases, i.e. affect one individual, not a group of people. This suggests it is going to be much more difficult to track down and control the problem since if indeed the food acted as the 'carrier' it could have become contaminated at any of several stages. The World Health Organisation Working Group on Foodborne Listeriosis view is that listeria is 'a widely distributed environmental contaminant', incidentally roughly one in twenty people are carriers, and that 'the means of transmission to humans is through contamination of foodstuffs *at any point* (our italics) in the food chain, from source to kitchen.' Sadly there has also been cross infection among newborn babies.

How many people suffered from listeriosis last year? The chief medical officer reckons that 'one in 7,000 known conceptions were infected' and in elderly people of about 75 years just 1.4 per 100,000. Exact figures are difficult not only due to under-reporting – listeriosis is not a notifiable disease – but also due to the fact that it may take up to 42 days for the symptoms to appear. In addition, a mild dose of listeriosis may appear to the person concerned just to be flu. However in pregnant women it may lead to stillbirth, premature birth, or even miscarriage. New born babies infected with the bacteria may suffer from meningitis.

Campylobacter – the unspoken hazard

While even those who are most concerned about listeria reckon the total number of UK cases including those undiagnosed was in the hundreds, a far larger number of people are *known* to be suffering from food poisoning as a result of the bacteria called campylobacter. There were 13,000 cases in 1982 and the figure last year is believed to have risen to almost 29,000.

Is campylobacter a food borne bacteria? When we spoke to the Department of Health they stressed that only a small percentage of the figures were linked to food, but Dr. J. Verner Wheelock thinks the evidence points directly to food as the culprit. 'There must be a *strong possibility* (our italics) that *most* (our italics) of the cases do originate from food.' One of the reasons to support this is the fact that you get outbreaks which affect a large number of people. What is the source of the infection? Links have been made to raw milk, milk that has not been adequately treated and, you guessed it, chickens.

Dr. Spence Galbraith, director of the Communicable Disease Centre and honorary senior lecturer at the London School of Hygiene and Tropical Medicine, said last year at a seminar run by the Food and Drink Federation, the industry's own body: 'two foodborne diseases have increased continuously throughout the 1970's and 1980's, namely salmonellosis and campylobacter enteritis. These are now the most important food borne diseases in Britain and require improved standards of hygiene in the preparation of food to bring about their control.' (1988).

Still more hidden problems

Although we have no published figures, according to Dr. Galbraith, two other foodborne diseases are also on the increase. He stated (1988): 'viral gastroenteritis and infectious jaundice (hepatitis A) conveyed by food also increased'. The source of these infections he said were 'often inadequately cooked shellfish harvested from sewage polluted waters'.

The list of food borne diseases does not end here – but rather than repeat a litany of various diseases for which we have no figures and some of which are thankfully rare in this country, we have decided to highlight one other organism which may indeed be a cause of considerable minor food poisoning. It is called bacillus cereus and is found in cereals, rice and other dehydrated foods. Its spores are already in the foods and some spores will survive cooking. If left for some time in favourable conditions they will then germinate into bacilli, which under warm storage conditions will grow and produce a toxin. It is this toxin which causes the violent vomitting associated with bacillus cereus. The toxins are extremely resistant to heat and can remain after being subjected to temperatures of up to 121°C for as long as one and a half hours. In this country most outbreaks have been linked to reheated rice, i.e. when say boiled rice is converted into fried rice. The symptoms are vomiting and diarrhoea within one to sixteen hours, and under-reporting is therefore likely to be even more common than with salmonella-linked infections.

Overall picture

So far we can say:

- food poisoning in this country is rising substantially at a high enough rate to be medically labelled an epidemic.

- the chief culprits are two bacteria: salmonella and campylobacter.

- the increase in salmonella outbreaks is linked to a new more virulent strain enteritidis type 4 which has been detected in both chicken meat and eggs.

- a common bacteria in our environment, listeria, can cause a deadly disease called listeriosis and has in some circumstances been linked to food.

- pregnant women are in the high risk category as far as listeriosis is concerned. Although the woman herself may think she has simply had a dose of flu, the effect on the foetus can be deadly.

- food may become contaminated with listeria at any point between production and consumption.

- food poisoning as a result of viruses, not bacteria, is also increasing and in some cases has been linked to poorly cooked shellfish harvested from polluted waters.

- a spore producing organism called bacillus cereus can cause minor food poisoning and is found in cereals and rice stored in moist, warm conditions for a considerable length of time.

Also,

- all food contains bacteria, many of which are either harmless or beneficial.

- roughly one in ten people in this country are probably carriers of salmonella and one in twenty are probably carriers of listeria.

- in normal circumstances we cannot eat sterile food since bacteria are all around us and live in us.

CHAPTER TWO:
WHY ARE THE BACTERIA WINNING?

The experts agree that more and more of us are getting food poisoning, so the key question is 'why?'. If we can answer the 'why', then we are half way towards putting the situation right. Broadly speaking three things may be happening:

1) The food we eat may contain more bacteria

This could mean either that our diets have changed so we are eating more of the foods which traditionally have always contained bacteria or there is a higher concentration of bacteria in our food.

2) There are new strains of bacteria

Generally it takes time for people to build up an immunity to new diseases. There tends to be a 'take off period' where infection spreads, then as the population as a whole builds up resistance the incidence of the disease decreases.

3) Our resistance to the bacteria has been weakened

Babies under two, the elderly, expectant mothers and those suffering from diseases, including AIDS, have reduced resistance to food borne bacteria. Therefore if the overall percentage of this group of people in the population grew, then other things being equal, the overall percentage of food poisoning incidents would grow.

As we will see the three factors are not mutually exclusive and therefore our present epidemic could be the result of all three things working together. As we have already noted it is incredibly difficult to trace back food poisoning to its cause so the evidence is likely to be circumstantial, but nonetheless we would argue it is a valuable exercise.

1) More bacteria in our food

If there are more harmful bacteria in the food we eat that's because more of our food is infected and nothing has been done to it before we eat it that will kill the bacteria. There is evidence that more of our chickens are now infected with salmonella than in the past. Indeed some experts reckon nearly two thirds of the chickens we buy for home cooking may be infected in some way, although the level is not likely to be sufficiently high to cause food poisoning in many cases.

No figures are available to show what proportion of our flocks is infected with salmonella and research is badly needed. There is some evidence that part of the problem can be traced back to a glut of cheap South American fish meal which was imported some ten years ago. The subsequent spread of the disease was accelerated by some farmers' habit of feeding dead chicken carcasses to their flocks and inadequate hygiene in some cases. There is also evidence that if you keep chickens in cramped conditions you increase the chance of cross-infection and thus speed up the spread of the disease within the flock.

Now salmonella is killed by heating to 63° Centigrade for half an hour. So since in theory we eat our chicken thoroughly cooked in this country we should not be at too much risk. True there are always going to be some cases of inadequate cooking – but if we are eating at home we should be able to confidently say we can kill salmonella.

What about changing eating habits? We now eat 500% more chickens than 20 years ago and in the last three years there has been a surge in processed chicken products, many of which we do *not cook* before eating them at home. For example, in 1987 roughly half the sales of processed chicken products in total some £77m went on ready-cooked and fresh items. Were all of these thoroughly cooked?, we do not know. There is some anecdotal evidence from environmental health officers that poorly cooked Bar-B-Qued chickens may be responsible for the increase in cases of salmonella in the summer.

So much for salmonella in poultry, what about eggs? As we have seen tests on a handful of flocks have shown salmonella to be present in both the chicken's oveducts – that's the passage through which the egg travels – and in some eggs themselves. There is nothing new in this. There was an outbreak of salmonella poisoning in pigs during the second world war that was traced back to the dried egg in their feed. So we really don't have sufficient data to back up a claim that this source of infection is increasing. As to the manner in which we eat eggs – that has not changed dramatically – and indeed the figures show we now eat less eggs than ten years ago.

What about the growth in food poisoning from

campylobacter? This bacteria is found in animals, foodstuffs, the soil and water. It may therefore infect farm animals, vegetables and fruit. The bacteria can be spread from person to person, animal to animal and is most likely to be found in raw milk, inadequately treated water and chickens. Relatively low concentrations of bacteria can cause illness. The trend towards organic farming could in theory lead to greater contamination of produce with this bacteria since the fruit and vegetables will not have been sprayed with chemicals to kill the bugs and may well have been grown in pig's or cow's manure in which this bacteria flourishes.

Campylobacter is killed by a heat of 100°C (212°F) for at least ten minutes. But then, most of our fruit is uncooked and our salad vegetables – lettuce, tomatoes, cucumber, etc. are eaten raw. Figures show we eat more fruit, vegetables and chicken per person than in the past.

Finally, let's look at listeria. Again this is found in the soil, in animals and humans. Unlike salmonella and campylobacter it actually likes a nice cool environment like a chill cabinet. It manages to survive at temperatures right down to 0°C, freezing point, and some experts argue it can flourish at as low as 2°C. So while refrigeration may have helped stop certain bacteria multiplying in our food it has only served to encourage others such as listeria. Listeria is killed by cooking food until it is 'piping hot' throughout and cooking by microwave may not destroy it completely *unless* the instructions are properly followed, including standing times.

The way we eat our food is also important. Ironically

the trend towards healthy eating has led to a greater degree of freedom for bacteria to grow in our food. Bacteria don't like heavily salted environments – but we now place less and less salt in our food products. Bacteria thrive in jelly – but not in fat. Yet, we now coat much of our meat in jelly, not fat. Bacteria hate sugar – yet much of our food now contains little or no sugar. So it turns out that what the experts regard as more healthy for us is also a healthier environment for unwanted bacteria. The addition of water and emulsifiers in our food which have again helped reduce the fat content – and in some cases appear to be used simply to inflate the manufacturers' profits – are two other features which help turn our food into a fertile breeding ground for harmful bacteria.

There is also evidence that our philosophy of 'eat and run' has been a factor. We have got tired of cooking food for ourselves and therefore buy more ready cooked food, some of which may be stored in conditions ideal for the spread of listeria. A survey by the Public Health Laboratory Service, published in the *Lancet*, found listeria in 12% of samples of pre-cooked ready-to-eat poultry and 18% of cooked and cook-chilled meals. Low levels of the bacteria were also found in pre-packed salads. It was not clear at which stage in the food chain the items had become contaminated, i.e. at the factory, on route to the store or within the store itself. Hence the government's concern for so-called cook-chilled products, which have recently been implicated in a *few* cases of listeriosis.

What about the great soft cheese debate? Listeria likes a nice warm, non-acidic environment. Most traditional British cheeses are of a dense consistency and not an ideal breeding ground for the bug. However, some of the newer brands and some imported cheeses are soft ripened and listeria can flourish in these. A recent UK survey found listeria monocytogenes in 14% of French cheeses, 4% of English and Welsh cheeses, 16% of Italian cheeses and 10% of Cyprus soft cheeses. So changing taste in cheese may well have contributed to the spread of listeria. By the way, it is important to note that there is no evidence that cheese made from non-pasteurised milk is more open to contamination than that from pasteurised. Hard cheeses, e.g. cheddar type, processed cheeses, cottage cheese and cheese spreads have not been found contaminated.

Although the listeria debate is new to many of us, it has been known for several years that soft cheeses heavily contaminated with the bacteria are dangerous. A year ago George Pinker, president of the Royal College of Obstetricians and Gynaecologists, warned of the potential dangers to pregnant women of eating certain types of cheese. Yet the general population had to await the Chief Medical Officer's letter of February 16, 1989. Sadly the warning came too late for Amanda Jupp whose story we tell in chapter nine. Amanda's baby Matthew was born with the disease – and we do not know how many others may have been saved if the Government had been more prompt in its warning.

So we can say:

● the evidence suggests a greater number of our chickens are infected with salmonella than 20 years ago.

● the facts show we eat 500% more chickens than 20 years ago.

30

- the evidence on eggs is unavailable.

- trends towards healthier eating may have contributed towards the multiplication of any food borne bacteria that were in the food *originally*.

- changes in the variety of cheese we consume may have increased the number of people getting listeriosis.

- poor refrigeration and bad food hygiene may have allowed more of our food to be contaminated with listeria.

- inadequate heating of food when using microwaves may have resulted in some listeria remaining in cooked food.

2) New strains of bacteria

It is always difficult to assess claims from scientists that they have discovered a 'new' disease. Quite simply, it is possible to argue that our powers of detection have improved and that the disease was there all along. That said, we have evidence of a new strain of salmonella and some scientists argue that its growth appears to reflect the worsening health of our poultry flocks. Incidentally, the National Farmers Union accepts that a new strain is at fault. In a statement on the 1st March 1989 it said: 'The NFU has never denied that the new strain of salmonella was a new problem which had to be tackled and we were co-operating in doing that.'

Our current salmonella crisis could then be a phase we

31

are passing through. A new bacteria develops, people fall sick, develop an immunity and gradually the disease looses its hold. This argument may hold good for the new strain of salmonella and even for listeria, but it does not explain the rising incidence of poisoning due to campylobacter.

So we can say:

- when a new disease emerges there is a standard curve, rising at first as the disease spreads then falling as the population build up their immunity.

- if listeria and salmonella enteritidis phage type 4 are indeed new food borne poisons, then the statistics are following a normal, if worrying, pattern.

- the spread of campylobacter is not explained by this theory.

- there will always be new diseases springing up and replacing the old ones which may obscure the longer term trends.

3) We are less resistant to infection

The subject of immunology – how our body protects itself from disease – is fascinating, complex and developing fast. Here again we are faced with an irony, the less we come into contact with a dangerous bacteria the more likely it is to knock us for six when we do. Hence, when we go to foreign countries and come into contact with what to our bodies are 'strange bugs' we are more likely to get sick than the natives who have grown up with those same bugs.

Whether as a nation we are less resistant to infection than in the past is impossible to say. The air we breathe, the water we drink, the stresses and strains of modern living will affect our immune system and will vary from individual to individual as well as in any one person from time to time. It may well turn out that all these chemicals are indeed reducing our immunity by making it more difficult for our bodies to obtain the vitamins and minerals required in sufficient quantities. However, the government's chief medical officer has repeatedly warned that certain groups are in the high risk category for food borne poisoning. Those at risk include the old, a growing percentage of our population, and those suffering from diseases which adversely affect our immune system, such as AIDS. So far the official statistics show just over 2,000 reported cases of AIDS, half of which have led to death. The number of people HIV positive but without fully blown AIDS – but with impaired immune systems is not known. So the number of people who qualify as members of the 'at risk' group is sadly growing.

So we can say:

- there is no evidence on the state of the immune systems of the general population.

- certain groups of people are in the high risk category for food poisoning and the number of people in some of these groups, i.e. elderly, HIV positive and AIDS sufferers is growing.

- hence a larger proportion of the population may be less resistant than in the past to food poisoning.

Returning to our original question, why are the

harmful bacteria winning, we can answer because we are making it easy for them to succeed. We are:

- eating more foods such as chicken, meat, fruit, vegetables, eggs where bacteria may be present.

- not taking adequate steps to prevent our food being contaminated with bacteria in the first place.

- not taking adequate precautions to prevent our food being contaminated between the time it is produced and the time it is eaten.

- eating our food processed in a way which encourages bacteria to grow.

- succumbing to new strains of infection.

- faced with a population where there is a growing number of high risk people.

Where do harmful bacteria grow

Type of Food/Drink	Bacteria Yes	No
Untreated water	●	
Bottled/filtered water[1]		●
Raw milk	●	
Heat treated milk		●
Home made ice-cream	●	
Commercial ice-cream[2]		●
Raw eggs	●	
Pasteurised eggs		●
Thoroughly cooked eggs (yolk firm)		●
Bread		●
Butter, margarine		●
Jams and honey		●
Seafood	●	
Raw meat and poultry	●	
Cooked meat and poultry	●	
Products containing meat/poultry	●	
Yogurt	●	
Acid fruits, e.g. apples		●
Fruit – the peel[3]	●	
Potatoes	●	
Salad vegetables	●	
Cooked vegetables	●	
Flour[4]	●	
Cream	●	
Dried foods	●	

Notes:
1. Some filtered waters may harbour bacteria if the filtration process has been inadequate, perhaps due to poor maintenance.
2. Provided pasteurised and handled in accordance with regulations.
3. Insects carry disease and may leave traces on peel.
4. In this country most of the problems have been with rice, since we use hefty doses of chemicals when storing flour to prevent bacteriological growth.

From the table it is clear that bacteriologically speaking the safest thing to eat is jam sandwiches washed down with pasteurised milk. Since man cannot live on jam sandwiches alone, clearly we need to take immediate action to beat the bugs. In the next chapter we look at ways we can start to fight back.

CHAPTER THREE:
HOW TO WIN THE BATTLE
OF THE BUGS

Having seen what's wrong with our food, how can we improve matters? We do not believe there is a magic wand which we can wave to rid ourselves of potentially harmful bacteria lurking unseen in our food. Instead we would argue that standards need to be improved in five key areas: farming, food manufacturing, food retailing, catering and level of regulation. We accept that these improvements will not happen overnight, that it might take three or four years to clean up our poultry flocks, a year and a half to get a new food bill on the statute book and a similar period to increase the numbers of environmental health officers monitoring the rules at the sharp end. But we believe that this package of measures taken together with better consumer care in the home (see chapter seven) should provide an effective answer to the current food crisis and ensure that in future British food is not only fit to eat but a source of enjoyment.

Before looking in detail at this package of measures, we feel a word should be said about irradiation. We have detected a growing body within the food industry, notably among some retailers and manufacturers who support the lifting of the ban on irradiation of food. For example, the industry's trade body, the Food and

Nutrition Federation says: 'Food irradiation is seen by British food manufacturers as a new sophisticated method of improving the quality and safety of food available to the consumer.' (A Revolution in Food Preservation.) Irradiation of food involves zapping food with radiation to destroy the live bacteria it harbours. So far it has been banned in Europe and the UK but the government is under pressure from scientists and some powerful food lobbyists to permit its introduction subject merely to adequate labelling so consumers know whether or not their food has been irradiated.

The push for irradiation is gathering pace because some food lobbyists see it as the easy and relatively cheap answer to the food bugs problem. Forget about trying to avoid contaminated food, just irradiate it before it lands on the consumer's plate they would argue. We believe this is simply the wrong way to tackle the problem and that insuffient research has been done on irradiation for us to tell what bombarding food with radiation does to its chemical constituents, and its vitamin content. We would also be wary about any promises by the government that it could guarantee greedy manufacturers made certain a sufficient time gap existed between the irradiation of food and it being sold to customers. In short, we feel the onus should be placed on those members of the food industry who wish to introduce this technique to do long term research to prove its safety. We would stress the words 'long term'.

In case some readers may feel we are being rather paranoid about the issue, it is worth remembering that one of the reasons hormones cannot be used in treating animals whose meat is sold in the EC, was because some farmers did not leave an adequate gap between injecting the homones and killing the animals for meat. As a result when some of the meat was eaten, people suffered a reaction from the hormone residues. Also, one of Britain's leading food retailers, Marks & Spencer, argue that what's needed is better hygiene not irradiation. David Elliott, at M & S, says: 'Irradiation is the wrong alternative to good manufacturing practices. It could be used to cover up contaminated food. The answer is to keep the food clean and free of contamination to start with.' His view is shared by the National Union of Farmers who on February 23, 1989 said: 'we believe that the adoption of irradiation as a means of preservation is *open to abuse* (our italics) and that measures must be taken to adequately regulate the use of this process.'

As we went to press (April 1989) it looked as if despite customer resistance and some retailers' objections the government was planning to lift the ban on irradiation. The timing of such a move appeared unclear, although as there is no need to incorporate it in the new food bill the ban could be lifted immediately.

What needs to be done

● Farming

Our poultry flocks needs to be cleaned up and rid of vast pools of salmonella infection. The quickest solution would be to simply kill the infected flocks. Experts argue that this would substantially increase the costs of our chicken and eggs, that it would be difficult to avoid cross-contamination and it would take two to three years to rebuild our flocks. The alternative is better hygiene, sterilised feed and a gradual decline in the level of infection which could take three to four years according to experts we have contacted.

We believe:

- infected flocks should be killed. A view incidentally shared by the National Farmers Union which said on March 2, 1989: 'we support compulsory slaughter of poultry flocks found to be infected with salmonella.'

- no compensation should be given to farmers whose flocks are infected. (A view not shared by the National Farmers Union.)

- in future, poultry should be fed with sterilised feed.

- eggs from flocks either proven or believed to be infected should not be permitted to be sold for pasteurisation but should be destroyed. Although pasteurisation should kill the bacteria there is always the possibility of inadvertently further spreading the disease, e.g. through cross contamination.

- veterinary inspection should be increased, so there is a lower likelihood of sick chickens being slaughtered and lapses in hygiene taking place during and immediately after slaughtering.

- the practice of feeding chickens with the remains of dead chickens should be halted.

- eggs should be marked so consumers and public health officials can trace the original source of supply.

So much for poultry farming, but what about cattle? In the current food crisis too little attention has been paid to the state of the red meat we eat. We have interviewed the chairman of the Public Health Committee of the British Veterinary Association, Mr Bill Reilly, and the picture he paints of the conditions in our slaughterhouses and the unwillingness of the current government to remedy the situation is in our view nothing short of a disgrace. What is particularly galling is that far higher standards of hygiene and animal care are in operation in British abattoirs whose meat is exported, than in those producing meat for our own domestic consumption.

We agree with the BVA that:

– a centralised meat inspection system policed by vets should be set up to monitor the standards in our abattoirs.

– that environmental health officers would be better employed working in the community ensuring that food regulations were being met, rather than working in an area for which their training was inadequate.

– that standards of hygiene in domestic abattoirs should be brought up to the standards set by the European Community.

– animals should be delivered for slaughter in a clean condition.

– animals should be kept at the abattoir for the minimum time practical before being slaughtered. Recent research has shown that stressed animals

41

have lower immunity to disease and may therefore fall prey more easily to harmful bacteria.

– animals should be properly identified so it is possible to trace its farm of origin.

– animals should be checked for signs of disease and those suspected should be subject to thorough veterinary inspection.

– accurate reporting of inspection before the animal is killed and of meat inspection subsequently is vital.

– meat should be inspected to ensure that residues of any drugs given to the animal are at acceptable levels.

– as few abattoirs have back-up for bacteriological research, so new facilities are required.

– new rules on hygiene and training for the staff to ensure they do not unwittingly cause contamination or spread existing infection.

– that meat inspection practices should be changed so that the meat is inspected for the type of harmful bacteria which are causing problems today, rather than testing for diseases we have succeeded in eradicating.

– that we should embark on an immediate renovation and rebuilding programme so that the buildings in which animals are killed are not themselves breeding grounds for disease.

– that proper care and attention should be placed on

inspecting animals before they are killed to avoid slaughtering sick animals.

- tighter regulations to avoid cross contamination between live animals and meat.

- an urgent regulation is needed, especially in light of recent concern about cook-chill and bacteriological infection, as are mandatory rules on the temperature at which the meat is stored, the length of time it is stored, and adequate monitoring and reporting procedures to ensure these conditions are met.

- there should be rules governing the loading and transport of meat – including temperature and time factors.

- that regulations covering the factors listed above should be passed to cover the killing, inspecting and distribution of all livestock including sheep, pigs, rabbits, chickens and farmed fish with detailed instructions on storage and distribution temperatures according to type of animal or fish.

- that the government should act now, not wait until 1992.

As we said earlier it is important that our standards cover not simply British farmers and manufacturers but also all imported food. In the case of animals the BVA brief which it prepared for the debate on this topic in the House of Lords on 9th March 1989 stated: 'It is quite plain that free movement of animals, which is a consequence of the Single European Act, will endanger UK livestock. The responsibility for health

43

status must be at destination and not just at source.' In plain English unless we wish to put our animals at risk of catching disease, we need to have powers to halt imports on health grounds. Otherwise we could see an epidemic sweeping our livestock. If this sounds unduly alarmist, consider the following: African swine fever has been present in cattle in both Spain and Portugal for the past 10 years; while the UK has not seen an outbreak of foot and mouth disease since 1981, Italy, Portugal, Spain and West Germany have all suffered from the disease over the the last seven years.

While on this question of infected meat, we feel the public should be aware of BSE – which stands for bovine spongiform encephalopathy. Sadly this tale seems to mirror the story of poultry. The main route of infection for cattle has been traced back to – you guessed it – infected feed. The Ministry of Agriculture, Fisheries and Food confirmed in March that 'the most likely source of the problem was feed containing sheep's brains.' Now BSE is a viral infection and cannot be treated with antibiotics – either in humans or animals. Infected animals have to be killed and their carcases burnt if the virus is to be destroyed. If any infected meat gets into the food chain – and the brains are likely to carry the highest concentration of the virus – the virus will remain alive and kicking throughout any processing since the meat will not be heated to a sufficiently high temperature to kill this virus.

It is difficult to track BSE infections since it may be several years before the illness – fatal dementia – becomes apparent. However, the government's figures show an alarming rise in cattle deaths as a result of BSE. The disease was made notifiable in June 1988.

The death tally was 42 by 13th November 1987; 532 by 10th June 1988; 1,036 by 23rd September 1988; 2,539 by 27th January 1989 and 3,745 by the 31st March 1989. By the end of March 1989 it had spread to 2,000 farms.

How has the government responded? Well, it commissioned a report which concluded that BSE was unlikely to be a risk for humans and has set up the Tyrrel committee to do further research. Mr Donald Thompson, the junior agriculture minister, told the House of Commons on March 16, 1989 that: 'The government planned to introduce restrictions on the use of offal in feed.' The government has told farmers to kill diseased animals but it does not insist on incineration of the carcase.

Here again the government appears to be waiting for people to get sick, before it will take action. It has banned the use of beef brains in baby foods, but not all food. In many ways BSE is a more important issue than salmonella for as H. C. Grant and William Blackwood, from Charing Cross and Westminster Medical School, pointed out in a letter to *The Times* on March 23, 1989: 'Unless bovine brain is totally banned from human food, or is *avoided* (our italics), a new human health hazard hovers over us, potentially far more serious than the various treatable infections we have lately heard so much about. It is the risk of *untreatable* (our italics) dementia.'

So how can we avoid eating beef brains, if the label on the food simply says 'meat products'? To be completely sure you need to steer clear of products such as pies, pâtés, sausages and Shepherd's Pie where meat offal may be masked by the processing.

We need:

- veterinary scrutiny in our slaughterhouses to detect early signs of BSE in animals.

- a complete ban on infected feed.

- further research into whether the virus is transmitted to humans.

- further research to develop tests for the viral infection.

- advice from the manufacturers as to what products contain beef offal as the label will simply say 'meat products'.

- a rule requiring all cattle known to be infected with BSE to be incinerated. The Ministry of Agriculture, Fisheries and Food says at present roughly one third of the diseased animals are buried in waste disposal sites which it claims means the virus cannot get into the food chain. We think it is better to be safe – and incinerate – than have to be sorry later.

● Food manufacturing

All the major manufacturers of food we spoke to agreed that regulation was needed to ensure that throughout the industry high standards of hygiene and distribution were met and adequately trained staff were involved in preparing our food. Quite simply there is a huge gap in the food laws of this country – anyone can set up in the food manufacturing business and although in theory they must comply with the current food laws, the laws themselves are in some cases inadequate and outdated.

Mr Harry Solomon, chairman of Hillsdown Holdings, one of the largest egg producers in the UK and a major food producer told us: 'I would support statutory regulation which was legally binding and subject to scrutiny and inspection.' He stressed that the regulations must apply to imports, pointing out for example that 15% of poultry bought in this country comes from abroad. Mr Solomon believes that the result of such regulations would be to drive out of business some of the cowboys who have been giving the food industry a bad name, while making sure that all manufacturers met the high standards practised by the best producers today.

At the moment, consumers have to rely on a) the food producer to impose high standards or b) the retailer who sells the goods to impose high standards. In this regard, Marks & Spencer was widely praised for its strict risk control procedures and scientific approach to food. It sets strict rules for all its food suppliers which must be met and excess food or food which is not up to scratch much be destroyed.

We talked to M&S to see what they thought should be done: 'we would support a system which licensed food production premises according to the type of product being manufactured,' they said. As we write the food companies are lobbying the government over the proposed new food bill, which will probably be introduced in 1990.

In terms of controlling the food manufacturers and producers, including poultry and egg producers and those manufacturing animal feed, we would like to see:

– before a building can be used to manufacture food

it must be registered and licensed to make sure hygiene rules can be applied. Some buildings may be constructed from materials which harbour germs.

- the license may be withheld until such time as any alterations required or additional safety features are completed.

- the premises should be regularly checked to ensure compliance is maintained at all times.

- the company/person running the business should be licensed to produce the range of products they wish to make. Food processes should be divided into categories so that regulations on handling, hygiene, inspection and storage can be made according to type of product.

- there should be regulations regarding the checking of ingredients to ensure they are in a suitable condition. Such checks to be properly recorded and any discrepancies traced to their source and reported to the authorities if they indicate a breach in other regulations, i.e. rules on infected meat.

- staff should be properly trained and supervised at all times.

- rules on handling food and storage, including temperature, time and cleanliness of equipment should be drawn up according to broad category of product.

- staff should be checked to ensure they are not carriers of infection and in high risk areas, to be defined in the new rules but to include cook-chill, should be required to wear suitable covering to avoid the possibility of human beings contaminating the food.

– adequate food inspections before leaving the building.

– rules on storage, including time and temperature, of finished product.

– procedures to be followed in case rules are breached.

– adequate marking of all materials so that source and date of manufacture can be traced.

– health officers to have unrestricted, immediate access to premises and contents. The power to impose fines for breach of regulations, stop the sale of food and ultimately withdraw licence for persistent offenders.

– rules on packaging to ensure this is sufficiently robust to remain intact until the food is required to be eaten. Inadequate packaging may mean the food can be contaminated by harmful bacteria in transit or in the shop.

– damaged stock should be reported to health officers with documentation on its disposal.

– health officers should have powers to seize and destroy damaged stock.

We asked the Institute of Environmental Health Officers (IEHO) and some of their members how they would react to our proposals. The IEHO told us that it would 'welcome the transfer of responsibility for inspection of animal feed producers, poultry establishments and egg producers' premises to local authorities'. They also welcome the idea of registration, not as an instant solution, but as a step in the right direction. The IEHO said 'it seems illogical that anybody can start a business to make or sell food without any sort of check being made on the conditions in which they operate or the general standards of hygiene they practice.

Roger Armstrong, chairman of the IEHO's Food and Education group stressed the need for greater training among people working in food companies plus tougher enforcement powers than at present. Although gaining access to food premises is not difficult he said, taking samples sometimes proves problematic. He would like to see a similar act to that for safety and health, giving environmental health officers powers of prohibition, i.e. to make a firm cease trading, and of imposing improvements by a certain date in order for the business to continue trading.

● Food retailers

You can buy food from a large supermarket, the cornershop, a market or even from the milkman. The standard of care and hygiene varies from place to place. In general, the leading supermarkets take greatest care of our food because they have the resources, manpower and high turnover of food. But, apart from the general rule of not selling food 'unfit for human consumption' they are free to run their businesses remarkably untramelled by government regulations.

We feel new legislation should cover the following points:

– all retail outlets selling fresh food should be registered and licensed.

– all retail outlets selling non-perishable goods, suitably defined in the rules perhaps to cover canned goods, sweets, drinks etc, should be registered and licensed only to sell these types of goods. They would then be subject to less rigorous standards than those selling perishable goods.

– premises should be approved and monitored at regular dates.

– rules on staff training, supervision and hygiene should be introduced.

– rules on the maintenance of the premises.

– rules on storage of goods, including in shop and prior to the food being placed for sale. These to include temperature, time and handling regulations appropriate to certain categories of food.

– rules on adequate inspection, monitoring and reporting of standards of food on sale.

– ban the sale of damaged canned goods and goods beyond their eat-by date.

– introduce more adequate labelling of both manufactured and fresh foods.

– introduce special provisions for cook-chill, including

temperature control and a provision that if the rules are breached the food becomes unfit for human consumption.

- regular checking by health officers of premises, staff, hygiene, distribution etc.

- ability of health officers to impose on-the-spot fines, have immediate access to any part of the premises and sequester samples/documents as required.

- shops to display license where public can see it.

- repeated breach of regulations to lead to license being removed.

- rules on what happens to food when it is removed from shelves to ensure it is not resold. The retailers should be obliged if requested to provide health officers with documentation to prove the food had been destroyed.

- if food becomes accidentaly sub-standard, perhaps through a break-down in refrigeration, then the health officer should be informed and given details of how it will be disposed.

- health officers would have power to order the seizure and destruction of sub-standard food.

- special rules will be required for market stalls and people selling food on an occasional basis.

- take-away restaurants to be subject to the same requirements as other retailers.

● Catering

You can open a restaurant in this country tomorrow and no one will ask whether you are qualified, whether your staff are qualified or whether your premises are hygienic. The responsibility for monitoring our restaurants is currently in the hands of the environmental health officers. They argue that they are overstretched and so short of manpower that they cannot enforce the laws which now exist and that the current legislation is too lax. The IEHO said: 'There is a shortage of 300 EHO's in England and Wales according to a recent Local Government Training Board Survey. In this situation routine gives way to crisis, and *few* local authorities can carry out *regular* inspection of food premises' (our italics). Staff shortages vary from place to place, for example the Thurrock Council in Essex stated in the *Financial Times* (April 5, 1989) that it only had ten environmental health officers instead of 14.

Roughly 40% of food poisoning cases are traced back to food eaten at restaurants, or other catering establishments. Since it seems unlikely that we eat 40% of our food at restaurants – the British unlike the French are not great ones for eating out – it seems fair to conclude that a meal eaten in a restaurant is more likely to make you ill than one eaten at home. The arrival of cook-chill and its use in a number of catering outlets means even greater care is required. We therefore believe the rules we have suggested for food retailers in general should be extended to caterers, who should also be subject to tougher regulations in certain areas. We would suggest these should include:

– adequate training and registration of staff to ensure
  that people working in the kitchens, backrooms etc.

are properly briefed and monitored on hygiene.

- proper storage of food and disposal of wasted food.

- requirements on the cleanliness of both kitchen utensils and glasses, plates, cutlery, etc.

- rules on display of food, i.e. salad bars etc. to ensure these are not a source of contamination.

- an indication on the menu if cook-chill products have been used.

- proper use and monitoring of oven, microwaves etc. to ensure food is heated to high enough temperatures to kill harmful bacteria.

- proper cold storage and temperature control of fresh foods.

- adequate separation, properly monitored, of raw and cooked foods.

- regular quarterly inspection by health officers.

- some control over the description of food on menu to ensure it matches contents and to exclude special claims unless these can be proven, i.e. low fat, vegetarian, low calorie, etc.

● Level of regulation

The food industry is big business, it is a highly profitable business and in this country is inadequately regulated. Clearly that is about to change. We have already looked at proposals for better regulation of producers, manufacturers, retailers and caterers, so here we wish to take a brief look at who should be overseeing our food industry and the basic principles which should be reflected in the new food bill.

We therefore believe:
- The Ministry of Agriculture, Fisheries and Food has lost public confidence and is seen as a mouthpiece of the food industry, not a supporter of the consumer. It should be replaced by a Ministry of Food, which should work closely with the Department of Health. Any activities of MAFF which did not fit comfortably within this new specification should be moved to the Department of Trade.

- Committees advising the new ministry should consist of independent scientists as well as industry members, but where possible the weighting should lean toward the independents. While some critics have argued it is wrong to include so many representatives from the food industry, we have found during our research for the book that the best quite simply do 'know' what they are talking about. They are out there, operating in the real world, facing and trying to tackle food problems each day and the government badly needs their expertise, time and energy.

- More information on the state of our health and our food should be made public. The statistics on food borne poisoning should not be confidential and monthly statistics should be published either by the new Ministry of Food or the Department of Health.

- The new curriculum in schools should include a health and hygiene course which should be compulsory.

– The responsibility for monitoring the food laws should be with health officers, specially trained, and they should have powers to search food premises uninvited and to take away samples, documents in the same way that our VATmen have powers of entry and seizure.

– Breaches of the new regulations should be made public and in serious cases, businesses should be closed down.

– We need better labelling of our food (see next chapter).

– There should be powers so that the government can introduce emergency measures such as banning the sale of certain foods, banning certain imports or insisting that manufacturers warn high risk groups without having to resort to fresh legislation each time.

– We need a better reporting system for outbreaks of food poisoning. If food is easier to trace – as it should be under the new regulations – then this benefit will be lost if food poisoning cases are not properly reported.

– The registration and licensing should be paid for out of the fees charged to the industry.

– The health officers should be subject to central government scrutiny and appointment, not local authorities. Their powers should be national, not local, since much of our food is manufactured in one part of the country and sold elsewhere.

CHAPTER FOUR:
WHAT ABOUT OUR WATER?

Just as food can act as effectively as a 'transporter' and breeding ground for bacteria which are harmful to human health, so can water. Obviously the standard of our water is vital. It is not just the purity of our drinking water which is important but water used to 'wash' fruit, vegetables, cutlery, plates etc., etc. and any water that may be involved in processing our food.

While we discovered that the facts about what's in our food are simply not known by the scientists in many cases, that is not the problem with water. Our water supply has to be 'wholesome' and should comply with the strict standards laid down by the EEC unless a permission waiver has been granted by the UK government. This is all about to change. If the government's plans to privatise the water industry in England and Wales go ahead without delay then our water supply *must* meet the EEC standards. If a supply fails to do so then the government will have powers to ensure either immediate compliance or compliance within a given period. It will become a criminal offence in England and Wales to supply drinking water which is unfit for human consumption.

From a consumer's point of view the issues with water are therefore: what do the water companies know is in my water which I don't?; are the standards set correct? and, if the standards are breached in such a way as to be a health risk, will prompt action be taken?

What's in the drinking water?

We rang the Department of Environment in March to see what we could find out about the state of our drinking water nationwide. They could not tell us the answer and said we had to contact the companies responsible direct. That's incidentally 29 statutory water companies and 10 water authorities. Since the water providers, referred to rather inauspiciously in the official documents as 'undertakers', are government owned why we wondered could they not tell us the facts? They simply could not, they said, but added that once the water companies and authorities had been privatised the government would be issuing public data on the state of our water. We can see no good reason why it needs an Act of Parliament to get the government to tell us about the state of *our* water.

Undaunted, we contacted all 39 water providers and asked them a list of questions about what is in our drinking water. We concentrated on three areas of public concern: nitrates, pesticides and bacteria. The results are in the table. The ten water authorities, which were created by the Water Act 1973, supply water to about 75% of the population in England and Wales. The map shows the areas of the country they cover. We had received only 13 replies by the time of going to press.

● lead
The EEC guidelines stated that the maximum

58

admissible concentration for lead is 0.005 mg/l. The Department of Environment admitted that this level was exceeded in parts of Scotland and that this represented a 'health problem'. The exact number of homes and people affected is subject to dispute but the local authorities are taking steps to remedy it.

According to the Scottish Development Department, background note dated 10th February 1989, fears that 20% of the population may be affected by above recommended levels of lead in water are 'misleading and alarmist'. Its own figures include 3-4%, i.e. 15,000 people in Edinburgh. It states that by the end of 1989 83 out of the 103 supplies due to be treated will comply with the EC lead directive but some supplies will not be brought up to scratch until 1992.

Local authorities have the power to inspect water pipes and if these are responsible for lead seepage into the water they can insist that householders change the pipes. This may cost several hundred pounds and those on low incomes may qualify for a grant. The department warns that D-I-Y filtration may be a hazard unless properly maintained, so at-risk consumers really have little alternative but to pay for new pipes.

● nitrates

The EEC guidelines states that the maximum admissible concentration for nitrate is either 50 milligrams per litre, i.e. 50 mg/l of NO_3 or 11.3 mg/l of nitrate/nitrogen. On the 10th April, 1988 the Department of Environment stepped up its campaign against nitrates. It withdrew previous so-called 'derogations', i.e. waivers, and asked the water authorities to review their arrangements and submit proposals showing how they would meet the EC guidelines at the earliest opportunity. As we can see from the table some companies are still in breach of the EC guidelines on nitrates.

● pesticides

The EEC guidelines state that the maximum admissible concentration for an individual pesticide is 0.0001 mg/l and for all *detected* (our italics) pesticides 0.0005 mg/l.

The European guidelines were set in the late 1970's and were based on what could be detected in our water at that time. Since then more sophisticated techniques have been developed and more individual pesticides can be detected. In August 1986 the Department of Environment issued the water authorities with guidelines on pesticides and placed maximum admissible concentration values of 0.03 mg/l for two herbicides, atrazine and simazine. This level is 300 times the European guidelines for any one pesticide.

As we can see from the table several water authorities have detected these two herbicides in their water. In addition, Thames Water in a briefing note on November 18, 1988 stated: 'Since *July 1985* (our italics) we have found levels of atrazine up to 0.5 ug per litre in groundwater derived supplies and up to 0.6 ug per litre in surface derived supplies. Levels of simazine found are up to 0.4 for groundwater derived and 0.3 for surface derived supplies.' 0.5 ug/l translates into 0.0005 mg/l; 0.6 ug/l into 0.0006 mg/l; 0.4 ug/l into 0.0004 mg/l and 0.3 ug/l into 0.0003 mg/l. As you can see the figures for Thames Water would not meet the European guidelines for either an individual pesticide or the total concentration of pesticides.

- bacteria

The general rule is that water must not contain 'organisms, or their products, which either constitute a risk to public health or would make the water unwholesome. There should be no coliforms in 95% of the sample, no faecal coloforms, no faecal streptococci, no sulphite reducing clostridia and no marked increase in bacteriological growth, i.e. colony count, in a one milligram water sample tested at both 22°C and 37°C. If there is a growth in the colony count it must be investigated.

- aluminium

Since March 1988 the European guidelines on maximum admissible concentration of aluminium of 0.2 mg/l must be measured on the basis of a single sample. There has been a great deal of attention on the potential health threat posed by high levels of aluminium in water. Thames Water in a note dated August 1988 from P. T. McIntosh stated that Thames 'do have some failures against the directives MAC' (MAC – maximum admissible concentration), and they are unlikely to be the only authority unable to match the guidelines at present.

- polycyclic aromatic hydrocarbons (PAHs)

From evidence we have gathered it seems clear that several authorities are unable to meet the EC guidelines on PAHs: including some samples from Thames Water. While many PAHs are not a health hazard, one of them benzopyrene, is known to cause cancer in human beings. Benzopyrene is found in cigarette smoke.

The EEC guideline is 0.0002 mg/l. Part of the problem

What's in the water

Name	Level of nitrates	Level of pesticides	Any bacteria
Anglian	Complies with advice of government chief medical officer. Some exceeds the EC directive limit.	Various pesticides at levels in some supplies in excess of EC directive but not at levels which are unwholesome	No comment given
Bournemouth	Surface water annual mean: 20.5 mg/l Chalk borehole annual mean: 23.9 mg/l Chalk well annual mean: 10.9 mg/l All figures as NO_3	None detected	Average colony count per ml 22 072 hours on yeast extract agar for 1988 surface water source – 7; count at 37 024 hours on yeast extract, surface water – 5
East Surrey	Vary from work to work – 'well within EC limits'	Small amounts of simazine and atrazine. On one occasion only, mecoprop. Amounts within DOE guidelines	'No harmful bacteria'
Essex	0.5 to 20 mg/l in raw water sources. Less than 11.3 mg/l in fully treated water	Atrazine, simazine and isoproturon	No coliform bacteria generally present
Hartlepools	'Low'	n/a	'bacteriologically satisfactory'
Lee Valley	The company has 58 sources. Two have exceeded the 50 mg/l limit on occasion and a treatment plant has been installed. The remainder have nitrate levels which range from 0 to 40 mg/l	Atrazine and simazine above the EC limit but within DoE guidelines. Certain organo-chlorines within the EC limit	No positive results
Northumbrian	Complies with EC directives	'not aware of any significant presence of pesticides in drinking water'	Complies with EC directives
Portsmouth	Within the range of 3.5-7.5 mg/l nitrate. Not in excess of EC limit of 11.3 mg/l	Not in excess of DOE limit	'Not normally present'
Rickmansworth	Between 9.7 and 38.1 mg/l as NO_3	Simazine and atrazine	No harmful bacteria
Severn-Trent*	'High and rising nitrates are a signigicant problem in the groundwaters'	Atrazine and simazine below EEC or WHO guidelines	0.09% of samples of treated water contained E. Coli and 0.44% contained any coliforms
Southern	'All Southern Water supplies comply with the directive'		
Tendring Hundred	Well below EC directive limits	Not in excess of DoE guidelines of August 15, 1986	No harmful bacteria
Wessex	'We constantly investigate and monitor the situation'		

Notes *From 1987-8 water quality report which was sent in answer to questionnaire.

for many British water authorities is that the pipes which carry the water are still lined with coal tar pitch which contains PAH. Although the use of coal tar pitch for lining pipes was banned in 1977, some pipes are still lined with pitch and the replacement recommended, bitumen, also contains PAH compounds, although at a dramatically smaller level than pitch tar.

So we can say:

- some water providers are exceeding the EEC guidelines on lead in water in Scotland.

- several water providers are exceeding the EEC guidelines on pesticides in water.

- some water providers are exceeding the EEC guidelines on aluminium.

- some water providers *may* be exceeding the guidelines laid down by the EEC for PAHs.

Are the EEC standards correct?

Just because we are exceeding the EEC standards it does not necessarily mean our water is unhealthy. Similarly there may be cases where the EEC standard for a particular chemical is not tough enough. The first point to remember is that the EEC standards were the result of a political process – negotiations between member states. The ruling on pesticides, for example, reflected the general belief that pesticides in water were a bad thing per se. The pesticide concentration levels bear no relation to World Health Organisation levels which have been assessed on the basis of scientific and medical evidence. Other levels, e.g. lead, aluminium and nitrate were based on medical data that was available at the time.

As consumers we must look at the *medical* and *scientific* data which is available and not be hypnotised by reams of EEC guidelines. In addition, although there may be no conclusive medical evidence, since experimental data is not available, we may prefer to err on the side of caution. After all in its report on Salmonella and Eggs the agriculture committee said: 'the government could not afford to wait for cast-iron evidence before taking action.'

Looked at from this stance what can we say about the evidence of our water.

a) aluminium

Is the fact that there is more aluminium in some of our water than the EEC guidelines specify a cause for concern? The medical evidence is divided. Unpublished research from the medical research unit at Southampton University suggests that aluminium in drinking water could be a factor in Alzheimer's disease (symptoms include dementia) but other scientists argue that the causal link has not been properly established. Incidentally it has been known since the 1970's that if aluminium was able to enter the bloodstream it could cause what was dubbed 'dialysis dementia'. The jury on the potential health hazard of aluminium in water is still out.

While a question mark hangs over the issue, we should ask whether it would not be wise as a precaution to ensure the EEC guideline on aluminium was met as a matter of urgency by all water authorities. For example, according to the Scottish Development Department, background note 10th February 1989, 'programmes for aluminium in Strathclyde were originally expected to be completed by 1996 but recent information indicates that this will not be achieved at present rates of progress. An updated programme is awaited.' Some authorities use aluminium when treating their water and an immediate ban could lead to untreated water contaminated with bacteria, which would be more dangerous.

b) PAHs

These are found in the water supplies in many areas of England and Wales. The government is apparently looking into the issue but it could turn out to be a *major* problem for the water authorities. If the water pipes have to be relined not only will this be expensive but it will take a number of years. When you think of the amount of iron piping criss-crossing underneath our feet it is clear this would be a mammoth and extremely expensive task. In England and Wales alone there is what the Water Authorities Association describes as 'a fine spider's web involving more than 178,000 miles of water mains that criss-cross villages, towns, cities and the countryside.'

When we questioned the Department of Environment on this matter they confirmed they had asked the water authorities to look into the matter just before Christmas 1988. The results of the individual findings are being analysed at present (March 1989) but the Department of Environment stated that at this stage (March 1989) it did not believe the costs involved would be significant when taking into account the overall cost of replacing outdated pipes, equipment etc.

The controversy over what's in our water is likely to hot up. The Department of Environment is discussing the EEC guidelines with the powers that be in Europe. In addition, however, it is proposing that a new list, the so-called 'red list' should be compiled of the most dangerous substances in UK water. Rules should then be drawn up, it argues, restricting the dumping of these substances either directly or indirectly into our water system. Further action perhaps banning the use of certain pesticides completely or restricting their use might be considered. The government also appears keen to introduce incentives to farmers to reduce the amount of nitrates they use to below so-called 'standard' practice and to introduces fines for those who use what is deemed to be excessive amounts of pesticides.

Comments on the Scottish Office consultation paper about the 'red list' were due by the 20th February 1989 and are being considered at present. The National Farmers Union has welcomed the idea of zoning in principle and said that the government's proposed voluntary pilot schemes will 'enable more effective judgements to be made on the nature of measures which will be required for agriculture to make a contribution to the reduction of nitrate levels' (March 22nd, 1989).

The aim is to update the 'red list' as and when new information is available. The list marks a major step forward in consumer protection and if the measures outlined in the consultation paper are adopted to minimise 'red list' substances in our water then it will mean the UK has higher standards of water than the EEC guidelines, not lower as is sadly the case all too often at present.

THE PROVISIONAL UK 'RED LIST'	EC Directive Adopted
Mercury	#
Cadmium	#
gamma – Hexachlorocyclohexane (Lindane)	#
DDT	#
Pentachlorophenol (PCP)	#
Hexachlorobenzene (HCB)	#
Hexachlorobutadiene (HCBD)	#
Aldrin	#
Dieldrin	#
Endrin	#
Chloroprene	
3-Chlorotoluene	
PCB (Polychlorinated Biphenyls)	
Triorganotin Compounds	
Dichlorvos	
Trifluoralin	
Chloroform x	#
Carbon Tetrachloride x	#
1, 2 Dichloroethane	
Trichlorobenzene	
Azinphos-methyl	
Fenitrothion	
Malathion	
Endosulfan	
Atrazine	
Simazine	

We reproduce the provisional UK 'Red List' (page 67) from the consultation paper on control of dangerous substances in water (Scottish Development Department 16th December 1988).

As you can see some of the substances labelled as the most dangerous in this paper after considering their 'toxicity, persistence and capacity for bio-accumulation', i.e. how poisonous they are, how long they remain in the environment and whether our bodies store them, are found in the drinking water of several water authorities. In addition the presence on the list of one substance banned completely in March 1989 (dieldrin) and another, aldrin, due to be banned at the end of 1992 suggests we need a more coherent policy on pesticide residues, taking into account both our food and water.

For consumers, it is clearly a matter of keeping an eagle eye out for government pronouncements, especially ahead of privatisation of water in autumn 1989.

The new era of privatisation

What will privatisation of water supply mean to the customer? So far the only message we have received loud and clear is that prices will go up. The water authorities have tried to explain that higher standards cost more money – but in terms of public relations that just makes us all wonder whether we have not been short changed on quality for the last few years.

The water bill is both complex and controversial – as we all know there's many a slip between cup and lip. For consumers it does have some plus points, as well as some provisions which, if implemented at a later stage, could be beneficial. But that's a big 'if'. Points to note include:

- companies will have to provide details of the quality of their drinking water to the public. This will be in the audited annual report – usually published some six months after the company's year end – and must include data of any breaches of regulation. From a customer's point of view the problem here will be the timing – we will know what state our water was in up to 18 months ago, not its current state.

- under the act there are detailed requirements on sampling and testing. The main problem from a consumer's point of view being the potential for discrepancies in lab testing and the acknowledged error rate of some tests, plus or minus 50% in certain cases. In addition, for what the Department of Environment calls 'technical and epidemiological reasons' no tests will be done for harmful bacteria as a matter of routine, only if the water supply is either 'suspected of transmitting disease', or shows signs of certain organisms whose presence may indicate harmful bacteria. (See case study, p. 152).

- if standards laid down are breached there is a complex range of actions as set out in table 7.1 of the draft guidance on safeguarding the quality of public water supplies, consultation paper, February 1989. Department of Environment and Welsh Office (see pp. 70-1). Only if there is an immediate health risk is immediate action required. 'How does the

Breach Of Water Standards – Proposed Procedure

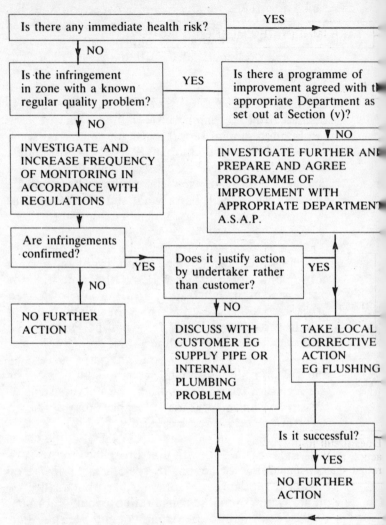

Source: Department of Environment and Welsh Office (February 1989) Table 7.1.

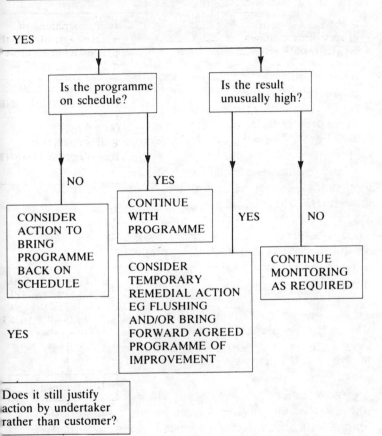

TAKE IMMEDIATE EMERGENCY ACTION

YES

Is the programme on schedule?

Is the result unusually high?

NO

YES

CONSIDER ACTION TO BRING PROGRAMME BACK ON SCHEDULE

CONTINUE WITH PROGRAMME

YES

NO

CONSIDER TEMPORARY REMEDIAL ACTION EG FLUSHING AND/OR BRING FORWARD AGREED PROGRAMME OF IMPROVEMENT

CONTINUE MONITORING AS REQUIRED

YES

Does it still justify action by undertaker rather than customer?

NO

Department of Environment define a health risk,' we asked. 'When people are sick,' was the reply. This surely is inadequate. There should be stricter rules stating health guidelines for the minimum standard of our water, which take into account the fact that some of our population suffer from reduced immunities, i.e. the old, the very young, the sick, and pregnant women.'

- the possibility of preventing potential pollution in certain vulnerable areas where boreholes and direct supply rivers may be open to contamination, i.e. water protection zones, is a good idea and one which most consumers, and it seems the water authorities themselves, support. The water authorities incidentally are on the same side as the consumer here – the less pollution, the lower the cost to them of clearing it up.

- the possibility of a pollution charge so that the polluter pays. Again both the water authorities and most consumers would be in favour of this provision.

- it will become a criminal offence in England and Wales to supply drinking water unfit for human consumption, but not in Scotland where the water industry will not be privatised.

- the government's plans to introduce a 'red list' of the most dangerous substances in our water and to implement a package of measures to reduce their presence in our water is to be applauded.

To sum up:
- the new water bill gives consumers a chance to have

a bigger say in the quality of the water they drink and how the industry which provides our water is organised.

- if consumers wish to control the level of pollution in water they should lobby their MPs in support of a 'polluter's tax' so that farmers or industrialists who dump toxic waste in our water supply pay the cost.

- if we care about our health we should press for guidelines linked to evidence of what substances in what amounts are harmful to us, rather than get obsessed by European guidelines which may be unrelated to health.

- the bill does not include a provision for consumers to know the state of the water they are drinking – only what they have drunk. However, it tightens up the reporting procedures, compliance requirements and penalties of any breach by a water provider of the guidelines.

- the bill does not include a provision for health warnings to high risk groups when standards are breached.

- the bill leaves the definition of public health risk undefined.

- the cost of complying with these new standards may be huge. Some estimates have been as high as £9 bn the figure guesstimated by EC officials quoted in a report in the *Financial Times* (March 1989). Although this figure was called an overestimate by UK government sources it raises questions about the decision by the government to privatise the water industry at this time as well as the question of how much consumers will have to pay for their water.

CHAPTER FIVE:
THE CHEMICAL TIME BOMB

While we may have some idea – albeit a gross underestimate – of the amount of people suffering from food poisoning as a result of harmful bacteria lurking invisibly in our food, we do not know the damage being done by the cocktail of chemicals we swallow along with our food every day. All our food, even so-called organically grown fruit and vegetables, sadly contains some chemicals. One expert, for example, told us that even if we decided to ban nitrates today it would be at least 20 years before you could expect our soil and water to be free of nitrates.

In this book we have tried to concentrate on the problem of potentially dangerous bacteria skulking undetected in our food. This is because we believe the experts who argue that bacteriological infection is the number one food related hazard at present. However, nobody knows the potential long term damage we may be doing to our health – and indeed, that of the next generation – by ingesting additives, pesticide residues and perhaps even banned hormones. It is not simply a matter of assessing the health risk of each chemical alone for the average person eating what is considered to be an average diet but also trying to weigh up the risks for particular groups, e.g. the elderly, young, pregnant women, and to assess the interaction between the chemicals. Nor do we know enough about our immune system to know whether this mix of chemicals in our air, food and water may be making us less resistant to other illnesses, including incidentally food related diseases such as salmonella poisoning.

As science advances our knowledge of what is safe – and equally important, what is not – will improve. While it may be excusable to put chemicals into our food when we cannot prove that they are harmful, it is clearly inexcusable not to use up-to-date modern methods of testing safety when these become available. But this is exactly what is happening today with pesticides. Many of the pesticides approved for use in this country have not been tested for safety for the past 20 years. The government announced in March 1989 plans to review pesticide safety of permitted products but said it would take 10 years to complete. This is plainly not good enough. Great strides have been made in science over the past 20 years, particularly in analysing chemicals which may cause or promote cancer. If the government has its way in ten years time we may discover that we have been eating food for thirty years that contains the residue of a pesticide which for example causes cancer. What's more there is a high likelihood that the residue will be found in a food we regarded and were told was 'healthy' such as fruit, vegetables, milk or bran, since this is where high concentration of residues are traditionally found.

We think there should be an urgent review of all pesticides in use in this country or used on foods sold in this country. Also, that the review should include tests for potential long-term damage to health and should take account of work done in other countries such as the US where several studies have indicated the link between certain pesticides and disease. While we accept that while this process is being carried on it would be impractical to impose a blanket ban on pesticides already permitted, we would like to see labelling of food – or signs carrying the information in the case of fresh food – so we know what pesticides have been used to treat our food. Plus, greater regulation of the use of pesticides which are permitted for non-agricultural use but which may still get into the food chain.

Pesticide residues in our food

Farmers in this country and throughout Western Europe rely heavily on pesticides to treat their crops and as a result much of our food contains pesticide residues. Ironically it is those foods which we have come to regard as 'healthy' which often contain the highest levels of residues. It is also virtually impossible to avoid eating the residues, for example peeling or washing an apple may reduce the residue level but not remove all the chemicals.

There are strict controls in Europe to limit the amount of certain pesticide residues in food but despite some breaches prosecution has been rare. The position in this country is rather complex. We permit the use of 400 or so pesticides but have statutory residue limits for only 61. According to the Ministry of Agriculture, Fisheries and Food 'this is because there is no evidence either that the others leave residues in our food or about the quantities'.

At least the situation is improving – but slowly. On

August 2, 1988 the government introduced legally binding maximum residue limits covering 24 pesticides used on cereals products and products of animal origin. On January 1, 1989, further regulations covering cereals, fruit, vegetables and fungi were introduced. Residue limits in animal feedstuff will not be introduced until December 3, 1990.

In November 1988 the Committee on Toxicity of Chemicals in Food, Consumer Products and the Environment recommended banning one of the pesticides, dieldrin for which limits had been set, and in the middle of March 1989 the government announced that all UK pesticide usage of dieldrin would be banned from the end of that month. Under the new rules the government has powers to seize and dispose of any food found to contain residue levels above those in the regulations and may also order 'any other remedial action as appears necessary.

So what do we know about the level of pesticide residues in our food? In March 1989 the government published the findings of the Ministry of Agriculture, Fisheries and Food working party on pesticide residues. It covered work done between 1985 and 1988.

As consumers we want to know:

- how much of the food that we eat contains pesticide residues.

- does any of the food we eat contain residues above the recommended guidelines.

- what is the government doing to improve any problem area.

• is there any way of avoiding food containing residues.

1) How much of the food sampled contained pesticide residues?

The working party looked at a wide variety of basic food and some processed food. Reading the report it becomes clear that although the majority of food sampled contained residues below the recommended limits, if these existed, a sizeable proportion of the basic foods we eat every day contain pesticide residues. It is worth pointing out that the report reckons the figures it supplies are within the range of 70% to 110% but 'ideally in the range of 80% to 100%'. So for any one item they could underestimate the actual residues by 30% or overestimate it by 10%.

We have compiled a table showing the percentage of key samples of foodstuffs which were found to contain residues **below** the recommended guidelines (see Table One). Those items starred, i.e. pulses, Scottish honey, peanut butter, were purchased from health food shops. Clearly the picture varies considerably, for example the figures for wheat suggest, according to the working party, that 50% of UK grain is treated with pesticides whereas residues were found less frequently in brown rice, rye products and processed oats. 68% of UK milk samples contained residues of organochlorine in 1985-6 but this figure had risen to 91% by 1987. Similarly 53% of imported butter in 1985-6 contained residues of this same pesticide.

Table One:
BASIC FOODS WITH PESTICIDE RESIDUES
OF PERMITTED LEVEL

Food	Year	Residue	Sample	Residue found but not above recommended guidelines
Offal	84-5	Pentachlorophenol	25	11
Poultry	84-5	"	25	9
Eggs	84-5	"	25	12
Milk	84-5	"	25	8
Pulses*	86-7	Bromine	176	136
Herb Teas*	86-7	"	39	8
Scottish honey*	85-7	Dichlofluanid	51	4
Peanut butter*	85-7	Organochlorine	40	17
Beef (UK)	84-5	Organochlorine and organophosphorus	120	15
Beef (imported)	84-5	"	20	6
Lamb (UK)	84-5	"	101	54
Lamb (imported)	84-5	"	59	27
Lamb (UK)	85-6	"	125	27
Lamb (imported)	85-6	"	50	25
Pork (UK)	84-5	"	140	18
Pork (imported)	84-5	"	21	0
Veal (UK and imported)	84-5	"	20	5
Chicken (UK)	84-5	"	122	36
Chicken (imported)	84-5	"	8	1
Turkey (UK)	84-5	"	30	7
Eggs (UK)	84-5	"	160	8
Milk (UK)	85-6	Organochlorine	176	119
Milk (UK)	87	"	120	109
Cream (Scotland)	84	"	7	7
Butter (Scotland)	84	"	11	11
Butter (Imported)	85-6	"	177	94
Cheese (Scotland)	84	"	20	20
Cheese (UK)	86-7	"	177	86
Cheese (Imported)	86-7	"	161	53
Brown flour	84-7	Organophosphorus	117	33
Brown bread	84-6	"	223	130
Brown bread	87	"	60	43
White bread	87	"	60	40
Bran	84-6	"	100	54
Bran	87	"	104	97
Bran-based breakfast cereals	84-7	"	151	14

Food	Year	Residue	Sample	Residue found but not above recommended guidelines
Wholewheat breakfast cereals	84-7	"	61	4
Wheatgerm products	84-7	"	44	24
Brown rice	85-6	"	84	20
Rye products	85-6	"	107	19
Processed oats	85-6	"	71	3
Malted barley (England)	87	"	136	82
Malted barley (Scotland)	87	"	83	60
Citrus drink	85	† Thiabendazole	48	26
"	85	† Phenylphenol	48	24
Fruit juice	85	Thiabendazole	12	4
"	85	Phenylphenol	12	1
Maincrop potatoes	87	Range of pesticides	75	47
New potatoes	87	"	45	18
Corned beef	85-7	Organochlorine	81	1
Minced or stewed beef	85-7	"	37	0
Tongue	85-7	"	21	3
Ham	85-7	"	80	2
Processed pork	85-7	"	78	18
Processed poultry	85-7	"	8	8
British sausage (uncooked)	85-7	"	177	52
Continental sausage	85-7	"	85	20
Burgers (uncooked)	85-7	"	150	72
Apples (UK)	85-6	Carbendazim	46	37
Apples (imported)	85-6	Diphenylamine	96	24
"	85-6	Ethoxyquin		10
Pears (UK)	85-6	Carbendazim	22	4
"	85-6	Vinclozolin		8
Pears (imported)	85-6	Diphenylamine	26	1
"	85-6	Ethoxyquin		3
Potatoes (UK)	85-6	2-Aminobutane	67	3
"	85-6	Chlorpropham		9
"	85-6	Tecnazene		51
"	85-6	Thiabendazole		13
White cabbage (UK)	85-6	Carbendazim	15	5
"	85-6	Iprodione		6
Lettuce	83-4	Range	81	52
Tomatoes	83-4	"	101	21
Mushrooms	83-4	"	120	15
Infant formulas	85&7	Organochlorine and organophosphorus	50	2
Rusks	85&7	"	31	18
Cereal-based foods	85&7	"	33	3

Food	Year	Residue	Residue found but not above recommended	
			Sample	guidelines
Meat-based foods	85&7	"	30	13
Egg, cheese or fish-based foods	85&7	"	14	3

Notes: * denotes purchased in a health food shop
      † no levels defined as MPR

2) Does any of the food sampled contain residues above the recommended EC or international guidelines or residues from pesticides not approved for agricultural use in this country?

In Table Two we have compiled a list of food samples which when analysed were found either to contain residues above the permitted guidelines or residues of pesticides which are banned in the UK or Europe. We have also highlighted what action if any is being taken. The main points to note are:

- Bromethane found in nuts and seeds bought from health food shops. Some tests have shown that bromethane is mutagenic – that means it alters our genes. The exact effect of this alteration is not known but it could result in babies with congenital deformities.

- DDT, banned in the UK, has been found in New Zealand lamb, poultry from the People's Republic of China, eels, and some fruit and vegetables grown in the UK. Although the figures for the UK fruit and vegetable residues are declining, that for eels raises the question of whether illegal use of DDT is occurring.

- Relatively high levels of dieldrin, which is not permitted for agricultural use in the UK, are finding their way into some samples of imported beef, UK chickens, potatoes and cows' milk. Since all these foods are basic items which we eat regularly in our diet there is a possibility that we may be eating more than the overall recommended level. In some studies dieldrin has been linked to cancer, allergies, and the birth of babies with congenital deformities.

- Organochlorine in excessive amounts was found in a few samples of UK milk, in some eels and in most samples of pork and poultry from the People's Republic of China. Permitted residue levels were also found in a wide variety of popular food stuffs, e.g. dairy products and meat. In studies, organochlorine has been linked to cancer and abnormal births but it is about ten times less toxic than dieldrin.

Table Two:
**RESIDUES IN EXCESS OF EITHER
EUROPEAN OR CAC GUIDELINES
OR FROM PESTICIDES BANNED IN THE UK**

Food	Residue	Excess residue (total tested)	Recommended action
Retail nuts and seeds*	Bromethane	18 (45)	Review
Lamb (New Zealand)	DDT**	2	Discuss with New Zealand government
Beef (New Zealand)	Dieldrin	1	Discuss with New Zealand government
Chicken (UK)	Dieldrin	2	n/a
Lamb (UK)	Diazinon	1	n/a
Lamb (UK)	Organophosphorus	2	n/a

Food	Residue	Excess residue (total tested)	Recommended action
Chicken (UK)	Fenchlorphos	1	n/a
Beef (UK)	Chlorfenvinphos	1	n/a
Pork and Poultry (People's Republic of China)	Organochlorine and DDT**	25 (26) 20 (26)	Discuss with People's Republic of China
Milk (UK)	Organochlorine	2 (176)	Try to trace source. Monitoring milk and surveying residues in animal feed.
White bread	Chlorpyrifos-methyl	1 (40)	Advisory Committee review advice on multiple treatment of grain.
Potatoes (UK)	Tecnazene	37 (67)	Review of use
Potatoes (UK)	Tecnazene	3 (120)	
Potatoes (Dutch)	Fluazifop**	10 (21)	Discussed with Dutch and agreed allowable residue of 0.1 mg/kg.
Apples (imported)	Bitertanol	3 (169)	Unspecified
Pears (imported)	"	7 (51)	Unspecified
Strawberries	DDT***	11 (236)	Trial to test residue level when use DDT on brassica crops.
Brussel sprouts	"	6 (92)	
Cabbage	"	7 (105)	
Brussel sprouts	"	0 (103)	No prosecution as not able to trace source.
Cabbage	"	2 (100)	
Brussel sprouts	"	3 (107)	
Cabbage	"	0 (118)	
Eels	Organochlorine and DDT		Monitoring.
Lettuce	Range of pesticides	14 (81)	
Tomatoes	DDT	1 (101)	
Mushrooms	"	2 (120)	
Peanut butter*	HCH †	17 (40)	
Unrefined sesame seed oil	HCH †	9 (13)	

Notes: * denotes purchased in a health food shop
** banned in the United Kingdom
*** DDT was completely banned in UK on 1 October 1984.
Not all residue levels found exceed EC limit
† HCH is banned in Europe on medical grounds

- Fluazifop. This is not permitted for use in this country since the Advisory Committee on Pesticides, whose job it is to vet pesticide use, said that if it were used the result would be an unacceptably high level of residue. It is used in Holland however, and the committee has now negotiated a permitted level of residue with the Dutch which has not been breached in subsequent samples.

- Biternol is banned from the UK since it was shown to produce abnormal births in laboratory animals. The residue level detected was lower than in the trials.

3) What is being done to improve matters?

The working party's report goes to the Committee on Toxicity of Chemicals in Food, Consumer Products and the Environment which advises the government on action to take. On the whole the committee concludes that the levels of pesticide residues found do not constitute a health hazard 'with the possible exception of certain imported meat and dieldrin in potatoes.' The government has introduced a complete ban on dieldrin since the end of March 1989 and plans to ban aldrin by the end of December 1992. The committee suggests monitoring the meat imported from the People's Republic of China, calling for *'firm action* (our italics) to ensure the absence of residues' and failing that, a ban on imports.

Among the committee's proposals are:

- support further work to trace organochlorine levels

in cows' milk which the committee says is a 'concern' since infants and young children may be exceeding recommended levels.

- a review of all use of bromethane.

- efforts to be made to reduce residue levels in infant food *as much as possible* (our italics).

- monitoring of sheep meat to ensure unacceptable levels of organochlorine are not present.

- monitoring of residue levels in bran which 'appear to be increasing' and the review of the multiple treatment of grain with a cocktail of pesticides.

- support for the review of tecnazene and recommends monitoring.

- monitoring of imported fruit for bitertanol residues to ensure no further increase.

- steps to identify and eliminate HCB (hexachlorobenzene) residues in UK milk, dairy produce, eels, meat and poultry. HCB is not an approved pesticide in the UK.

- review of precautions taken in premises where food is stored and handled to prevent accidental contamination of food. This latter responsibility is in the hands of the Ministry of Agriculture, Fisheries and Food and the Health and Safety Executive.

Is this good enough? As we have already seen there is some doubt about whether all the pesticides we permit to be used in this country are in fact safe and this report now shows that residues from banned pesticides and residues which exceed international guidelines are in some of our food. Has the government banned that food? Tracked down the culprits? Apart from trying to trace the source of DDT, it has not. Instead the government has discussed the matter with the Dutch, Chinese and New Zealanders. It has negotiated levels somewhere between what was in the food originally and our supposedly scientifically and medically based view that the residues should not be there at all. As for the question of Chinese meat this issue dates back to 1985 and we still import contaminated meat.

We believe, the government should:

- announce an immediate ban on contaminated meat from the People's Republic of China.

- ban residues in baby food within a stated period.

- track down anyone still using DDT in this country and prosecute them. DDT residues in eels from Culroy Burn, Rivers Eden and Ugie suggest current use of DDT.

- ban imported fruit with bitertanol residue.

- track down and prosecute anyone using HCB, which is not an approved pesticide in this country.

- ban the use of aldrin to treat potatoes straight away – not wait until 1992. It is reckoned to be four times more toxic than dieldrin and is banned in several countries.

- ask the committee to draw up guidelines for total

pesticide residues where the individual pesticides are similar in chemical constituents.

- introduce a system of certification of residue levels for meat and poultry which would be administered by vets at slaughterhouses.

- announce the results of reviews into fruit and vegetable based infant foods at the earliest opportunity.

- announce the results of the review of animal feed at the earliest opportunity.

- start immediate testing of mother's milk.

4)   Can we reduce the residues we consume?

Apart from avoiding foods which featured in Table Two, what else can we do to minimise our intake? Here's a few tips:

- low fat milk contains less residues than full fat.

- choose low-fat cuts of meat and remove visible fat.

- refined vegetable oils contain less residues than raw oils.

- wholemeal flour contains less residue than bran.

- organically grown cereal products contain less residue than ordinary cereal products.

- granary and germ-enriched bread contain less

residue than wholemeal or wheatmeal bread, even if the latter is marked 'organic'.

- organically grown pulses have less residue than ordinary ones.

- fruit juice made with the whole fruit has *higher* residue than that made from just the fruit itself.

- brown rice, rye and processed oats have low residues.

- new potatoes have slightly lower residues than old.

- corned beef and ham products have less residues than beef burgers and sausages.

- wholemeal babies' rusks have *higher* residues than ordinary ones.

- you can *reduce* but not eliminate the residues in fruit by peeling them.

- products purchased at health food shops are likely to contain the same level of residues as those purchased elsewhere.

- in terms of salad vegetables, lettuce has one of the highest residues.

Note: the above is based on the working party's report, looking at the percentage of each sample which had a residue detectable and on comments made in the report.

Additives

Most consumers could be forgiven for thinking they are told just about all there is to know about additives in their foods, thanks largely to our European cousins and their E codes. Sadly this is not the case. The main exclusions which cause concern are:

● natural additives and flavourings

Just because the original source of an additive is present in nature this does not mean that its derivatives are necessarily safe. As we all know only too well poisonous substances can live in natural products. We would therefore like to see this group of additives be subject to the same screening system as artificial ones.

● additives used solely as processing aids

these include enzymes and vegetable oils which are used when a food is processed but are not strictly speaking an ingredient.

● additives which act as a carrier for other additives

You can't just chuck in a dash of an additive and expect it to spread evenly throughout the food, you need to add – you guessed – another additive to do this job. This is called a solvent because it absorbs the first additive and then spreads it evenly through the food. Ironically you may end up eating more of the solvent than the original additive.

● additives in what's called 'single ingredient foods' and exemptions

If you add flour, alcoholic beverages, honey or cheese to your product you don't have to list any additives which they may contain.

- ingredients within ingredients which serve 'no significant technological function in the finished product'

So for example, if you make a cake with dried fruit treated with sulphites, that does not have to be declared.

There is wide scope for adding additives which we have no idea about. You could pick up a cake and it could be labelled additive free, yet its ingredients – the flour, dried fruit, flavours, fats could all contain additives. Clearly we need to be told and informed in a manner which is easy to understand. If an additive remains in our food when we buy it, then it should be quoted – regardless of the path it took to get there.

Finally, flavourings. Our food labels must state they have been used – but do not need to name them. If nobody knows what's used how do we know whether they are safe? The government's own leaflet on food labelling simply says: 'the European Community is now attempting the difficult task of regulating flavourings'. A first step would surely be to print their names on the labels.

Now it must be stressed that many additives perform a very useful function – they prevent the growth of dangerous bacteria which can cause food poisoning. So it is arguable that in our desire to eat additive free food, or at least food which we believed to be free of additives, we have ended up with products which go off more quickly and where dangerous bacteria can flourish more easily. In this sense so called 'healthier' and 'natural' food may in fact be more dangerous. Clearly if we wish to buy food free from preservatives we should treat it with greater care than the same food containing preservatives. We need to pay particular attention to sell-by dates, eat-by dates and storage. Also stick to shops with a high turnover and good hygiene policies.

Several books have been written on the potential problems which specific groups of people, i.e. hyperactive children, those prone to allergies, etc., may have if they eat food with certain E code additives. It is now possible to refer to a databank which lists many foods which are additive free. The food industry in association with the Royal College of Physicians has developed a databank of manufactured food products which are free of certain ingredients and additives which have been linked to health problems in a minority of people. Although this cannot be consulted by members of the public, it can be used by dieticians, doctors and qualified medical staff.

However, what we have yet to assess is the potential danger in using additives and flavourings derived from natural products. More and more of these are being used since they do not have to be printed on our food labels. Rigorous testing is required and they too should be declared on the label so we know exactly what is in our food. We have less information on the potential poisonous nature of so-called 'natural' colours than artificial ones and research is clearly needed.

Coming soon . . .

The EEC and the UK have banned the use of

hormones for livestock after evidence of their misuse in a number of European countries. However in November 1987 the general secretary of the Irish Veterinary Union went on record as stating his belief that more than two-thirds of meat produced in Ireland could have been treated with hormones. There is now a renewed move by farmers in some European countries to re-introduce hormones and this lobby has been strengthened by the report of the Lamming Committee which said that *under certain conditions* the synthetic hormones trenblone and zeranol were safe. If the findings of this committee are accepted strict control and monitoring of the synthetic hormones would be required, preferably in our view with veterinary supervision and we believe proper labelling of all meat and meat products produced from animals treated with these drugs.

Another new animal drug which is being considered by the EEC is Bovine Somatropin, called BST for short. This is being tested in the UK at present and, although no decision has been reached, milk from BST cows has gone into the common 'pool' for consumption. When asked by the Labour MP for Cardiff, Mr. Rhodri Morgan, whether milk from BST cows would be labelled as such the agriculture minister replied that this would be impractical. So we may be drinking milk from cows who are being fed BST when this synthetic hormone has not been properly vetted and passed. We believe this is unacceptable and that milk from BST cows should not be sold to the British public unless and until the hormone has been cleared as safe. A growth promoter for pigs called Porcine Somatotropin which has not yet been approved in the UK. However, it could be used in Europe.

It's the way they tell it

Our government's policy on food contents and ingredients is 'that, for most foods, having the information that you need about the product on the label is more important than restricting variety by controlling the details of the ingredients' (MAFF: Look at the label). We would argue that our labelling is inadequate and we are not given sufficient information in order to make an informed decision about what we are buying.

We would like to see:

● a full listing of additives plus an indication of their purpose.

● the date the product was made.

● an 'eat-by' date, regardless of whether or not it is a product with a shelf life of more than 18 months (i.e., to include cans).

● country of origin.

● an indication that ingredients are listed by weight.

● method of manufacture or process.

● full nutritional analysis.

● amount of water in product in percentages, not by reference to an EEC standard.

● what, if any, pesticide has been used.

- a proper description of ingredients, in the case of meat or fish to indicate which type has been used and which part of the animal/fish. At present, 'meat' covers liver, brains, fat, skin etc.

- datemarks on cheese, bread, poultry, sweet foods.

- standardised compulsory star-marking system on frozen food.

- labelling of cook-chill foods highlighting the need for care in storage and cooking.

- full name and address of manufacturer/packer/seller.

- the term 'natural' is misleading and should not be permitted.

- the introduction of maximum antibiotic residues in the EEC and UK, alongside better labelling to indicate their presence.

So what does this add up to?

Looking at the overall picture, what does the chemical cocktail of pollutants in our air, pesticides in our food and water add up to? Research is obviously badly needed but we talked to Foresight, The Association For The Promotion of Preconceptual Care. They argue that in today's environment to be healthy it is not simply sufficient to follow sound dietary advice. They say the chief causes of nutritional deficiencies include:

'a) The pill which manipulates the hormonal levels and

induces losses of zinc, B6, B2, Folate, B12, Vitamin A and manganese.

b) The copper IUD which squanders zinc and B6.

c) Heroic slimming regimes due to the weight gain induced by hormone manipulation.

d) Some food additives such as tartrazine induce the loss of B6 and zinc via the urine, and probably disrupt the metabolism of other nutrients also, we (Foresight) are presently helping to fund further research into this.

e) Fluoride, from water, toothpaste, drops and pills, is known to lower levels of magnesium.

f) Heavy metals such as lead from the atmosphere, mercury from dental amalgams, cadmium from cigarettes, and lead and aluminium from the drinking water can drive down levels of essential nutrients.

g) Organophosphate pesticides (used heavily in agriculture and timber treatment, mothproofing, greenhouse work, domestic fly killers etc.) are known to disrupt choline metabolism. Choline is necessary for essential fatty acid metabolism, and for the transfer of manganese across the gut wall. Essential fatty acids are involved in zinc absorption, and thus these chemicals may induce deficiencies of choline, EFAs, manganese and zinc.

Junk food is, of course a problem; so is the exhaustion of the soil subjected to inorganic farming and market gardening practices, which therefore renders the produce less rich in essential minerals. Refining of flour and sugar reduces the content even more.'

So as well as some chemicals being dangerous at certain levels they may also result in vitamin deficiences and disrupt our metabolism. This in turn may leave us less resistant to other infections including food poisoning and may even make a successful pregnancy less likely. In other words our food may be damaging not just our health but also that of the next generation.

CHAPTER SIX:
SHOPPING HINTS

How can you protect yourself when shopping? This is vitally important since it seems likely that the steps taken to clean up our meat, poultry and eggs will take at least two to three years and that it may well be the end of 1990 before we have a new food bill on the statute book.

Where to shop

Since at present we cannot rely on the government to police our food producers and manufacturers, we need to shop at outlets where the retailer is active in regulating the standard of products sold and where their own standards of hygiene are the highest possible. In broad terms this narrows down to a handful of high-street food retailers.

Places to be wary of: fresh food sold from non-food shops as a sideline; the corner shop unless you are sure it is run to very high standards; markets. Tell-tale signs would include: the sale of damaged food, poor hygiene habits, i.e. perhaps permitting smoking or animals, and badly ventilated premises.

Fresh food

There is no definition of fresh food in the Food Act and no rules on how long food may be displayed for sale before it is regarded as unfit for human consumption. Ideally you want to shop in the store which sells the freshest food in the best condition, but sadly, this is almost impossible to work out. We have sell-by dates or even best-before dates, but no one tells us when the food was made, manufactured etc. The exception is eggs as the packet does tell you the week they were packed, but not when they were laid. We think consumers should be told when a food was produced as well as the eat-by date, which will be introduced by 1992 in this country to bring us into line with European practices.

A quick sortie around a few high street supermarkets shows that each one has a different idea of how long food keeps fresh. Sandwiches may be sold in some places for several days, in others for just one day. We asked Marks and Spencer who say they believe they operate the shortest keeping lives to tell us some more information about the food they sell. The results are in the table.

So the bread you buy in the shops on Monday, will have been made that morning and M&S recommend you eat that day. The tomatoes will have been picked in the Canaries on say Monday, transported to Britain, find their way onto M&S shelves on Wednesday and will be sold by Saturday. It is then up to us to decide when we eat them by. The strawberries picked in Israel will also be on the shelves by Wednesday, sold by Friday and we are told to eat them within 24 hours of purchase. Cannelloni is produced on Monday, in the store the next day and must be sold by Saturday and eaten within 48 hours of purchase. Interestingly while both the lamb and fish are produced and delivered to the stores in 24 hours, the sell-by date for the meat is Friday and for the fish Saturday. M&S sell no damaged cans and food beyond its sell-by date is removed from the shelves.

MARKS AND SPENCER PRODUCT TABLE

Product	Prod/ Packed	In Stores	Sell-By	Customer Life
Crusty Bread	Mon	Mon	Mon	Mon
Canary Tomatoes	Mon	Wed	Sat	Not specified
Israeli Strawberries	Mon	Wed	Fri	Within 1 day of purchase
Cannelloni	Mon	Tues	Sat	Within 2 days of purchase
Lamb*	Mon	Tues	Friday	Within 2 days of purchase
Plaice Fillets*	Mon	Tues	Sat	Within 1 day of purchase

*Packed in controlled atmosphere packaging.

Points to watch:

• avoid shops where you find food past its sell-by date. It's not illegal but a sign of sloppiness.

• avoid damaged cans and shops which sell them cheaply.

• avoid food which has been in the sunlight.

- check staff working in shop are handling food correctly. Raw meat/fish should be separate from cooked goods on deli counter. Knives, cutting machines should be washed each time. Staff should not handle money then food – as paper money may be a source of bacteriological infection.

- if the food is 'off', report the matter to your local authority Trading Standards Officer or your 'environmental health officer and complain loudly in the shop itself.

- if you suspect a food has made you ill, keep a sample for testing. Make some notes on where it was bought, when and who ate it. Make sure you tell your doctor and environmental health officer.

- if you see a member of staff ignoring basic hygiene rules, don't shop there but write and complain to the store's owners, sending a copy of your letter to your local Standards Officer, environmental health officer, local radio station and local newspaper.

- form your own local 'action' group and monitor the stores in your area.

Cook-chill – potential hazard

Nearly half a million packs of cook-chill food are sold every day in this country. They are bought by consumers as well as by restaurants and hotels who use them to augment their menus. They are served to patients in hospitals. Are they a hazard to our health? Professor Lacey argues that due to inadequate care in the shops many cook-chill products are being kept at temperatures which permit listeria to multiply. The products he argued were then a health risk.

But is this true? As far as we can track down there have been no outbreaks of food poisoning in hospitals using cook-chill products, so that seems to imply the process itself, if completed with due care to hygiene and proper bacteriological testing, is not inherently dangerous. The trouble arises when the food reaches the store chilling cabinet, if it is not properly sealed then listeria can get into the product *and* if the temperature is not below 4° Centigrade the bacteria can multiply very quickly. In some experiments listeria has survived and multiplied at refrigeration temperatures down to 0°C.

If you take the food home and put it in the fridge at between 1°C and 5°C then off we go again, listeria will start multiplying. Listeria is killed at high temperatures, i.e. 70°C. When the Public Health Laboratory Service (PHLS) examined samples of cook-chill products those that it did find contaminated with listeria had a very low level of bacteria, i.e. 100 micro-organisms per gram. The director of PHLS has said that 10,000 micro-organisms per gram is the level at which a health risk occurs.

So what can we do to protect ourselves:

- buy food where you are confident the product has been cooked, handled and stored with care. This should minimise the possibility of initial infection.

- do not buy food which is unsealed, open to the air. It may have left the manufacturer uncontaminated but as a result of poor hygiene harmful bacteria could have grown in the meantime.

- do not buy food from cabinets which are stacked high. This means the temperature may be uneven.

- try to buy your food early in the day, as soon as it has been delivered.

- check sell-by dates and eat-by dates.

- take the food straight home and keep at correct temperature. You can buy a special bag for frozen products which will keep the meal cold.

- either eat straight away, making sure to reheat thoroughly or store in your freezer, if advised on the pack.

- if you are in the high risk group for listeria, cook your own meals, avoid soft cheeses, cook-chill meals and pre-packed salads, wash all vegetables and salads, and take medical advice.

- never reheat the meal more than once.

- eat the food the moment it has been cooked.

- if heating the food with a microwave make sure you follow the instructions properly, err on the side of caution and overheat if worried. Always allow the recommended standing time as that is part of the cooking time. Use a food thermometer to check for 'cold' spots.

The government is currently working on new guidelines for cook-chill products. The current guidelines were introduced in 1980 before the listeria scare.

They state food should be cooked and then chilled to 3°C within one and a half hours of leaving the cooker, where the food may remain for up to 30 minutes. The food must be stored at temperatures of between 0°C and 3°C for no longer than five days and subsequently reheated to 70°C. As we have seen listeria can grow at temperatures right down to 0°C so these guidelines urgently need reviewing.

Some local authorities are increasingly concerned about the potential threat of listeriosis as a result of contaminated cook-chill meals served to patients. Hospitals no longer have crown immunity so if an outbreak of food poisoning occurred and if its source could be traced to contaminated meals then a local authority could be sued. As a result some authorities are investigating conditions in the hospitals under their jurisdiction in order to ensure the patient's meals are indeed safe. At least one authority in London has found that some hospital meal samples showed signs of coliform organisms which indicated poor food handling at the manufacturer and could have indicated the presence of listeria.

Retailers are also looking at their refrigeration facilities and assessing the implications if they are required to store food at temperatures just above freezing. One retailer told us such a requirement would mean the installation of many new refrigeration cabinets since the temperature in most current models fluctuates by around 2°C.

Clearly we need:

- an immediate update of the government guidelines on cook-chill to take account of the new knowledge we have on the growth and survival of harmful bacteria.

- monitoring and testing of all hospitals and other institutions using this system.

- given that hospitals are of particular concern since any harmful bacterial contamination could lead to a large number of deaths, they should be subject to frequent independent monitoring by health officers.

- suppliers and distributors of cook-chill should be subject to strict regulations as stated in chapter three.

- manufacturers of refrigeration facilities should research and develop appropriate products.

- to examine the feasibility of a register of approved suppliers of cook-chill products.

Fresh food

In the following pages we have put together some shopping tips when buying fresh food. They have been based on our conversations with retailers, scientists, food manufacturers, the government's own report on pesticides (March 1989) and material from the British Food Information Service Publication: 'Prodfacts 1988' whose author Daphne MacCarthy kindly gave us permission to use data from her book.

Item	Shopping Tips

Item　　　　*Shopping Tips*

Apples　　　Stick to smaller sizes as the experts reckon these have better flavour. This goes for Cox's Orange Pippin, Egremont Russet, Discovery, Spartan, Idared and Worcester Pearmain. Avoid bruised or overripe fruit.

Alfalfa sprouts　　These have been linked with recent outbreaks of salmonella. Avoid if you are in a high risk category and only buy if you know they are fresh and you can trace the manufacturer.

Bacon and ham　　Check the water content printed on the label of pack or displayed near the counter if buying bacon by the slice. Look out for the so-called Charter Mark, short for the British Charter Quality Bacon symbol, on pre-packaged items. About 60% of British bacon meets this standard. To qualify both the bacon plants and the products manufactured must meet certain tests involving quality, hygiene and presentation.

Beans　　　The pod of a broad bean should be soft and tender. French beans should be crisp and juicy. A fresh runner bean will break cleanly. Avoid any beans which are deformed, damaged by insects or covered in clumps of soil.

Beansprouts　Same advice as alfalfa sprouts.

Beef　　　　Don't be misled by the colour of the meat

or indeed of the fat. Meat is bright red when first sliced but in order to improve its flavour is usually hung for several days. It should look slightly moist and lean cuts should have a smooth surface. The fat should be white or creamy white. Sad to say you need to buy meat with care. The state of many British abattoirs leaves a lot to be desired. Stick to reputable retailers with strict quality control, high standards of food handling, packing and store care. Avoid beef offal due to the potential contamination with BSE.

Broccoli   Check carefully for quality. Avoid any vegetables with yellowing leaves. Make sure the outer leaves and stalks are firm.

Brussel   Don't worry about whether they are dark
sprouts   green or light green – it simply depends on the variety. Check the base stalk is white, avoid those with loose leaves or yellow tinges.

Butter   Buy your butter weekly and check the date stamp.

Cabbage   Start your inspection by looking at the base of the stalk. It should be nice and firm. The outer leaves should look fresh and undamaged. If you buy unwrapped green cabbage avoid any vegetables which have been stripped of their outside wrapper leaves. Red cabbage should be tightly furled and avoid any with tell-tale dark brown patches. White cabbages should be chosen with particular care as these are often stored for a considerable time before reaching our shops. No-no's include brown smudges on leaves, 'relaxed' outer leaves and limp looking specimens.

Carrots   Go for the fresh, bright coloured, undamaged vegetables. Tell-tale signs of poor quality include: wrinkles, brown tips or squidgy bits. If buying pre-packed carrots, check date stamp.

Cauliflower Stick to medium sized heads with tight 'flowers', preferably creamy white. No-no's include those with: murky brown speckles, dirty stalks, browning stalks or separating 'flowers'. A slight yellow tinge is usually a sign that the vegetable had to put up with poor weather conditions.

Cheese   Fresh cut cheese should look fresh with no hard rough areas or sweat beads. It should have been stored at correct temperature and be handled hygienically. If you buy pre-cut packaged cheese, check the packet for signs of mould, moisture or greasiness. Any of these factors show that the cheese has been stored at too HIGH a temperature and should be avoided. Check the date code on the label. For higher quality cheese, look out for the Cheese Mark which covers about 80% of English and Welsh cheeses (excludes Stilton) – but since cheese can deteriorate during storing, handling, etc. you need to be very careful when making your final choice. In Scotland there is the Scottish Cheese Mark. If you are in the high-risk group you should avoid soft ripened cheeses. See chapter eight.

Cherries   Avoid unripe, split or diseased fruit. Also make sure that you are paying for the fruit, not inedible foliage. Cherries are usually sold with stalks attached but you don't want to buy the twigs as well.

Chicken   WATCH OUT – SALMONELLA IS ABOUT. If choosing a frozen bird then make sure it is unbruised, undamaged and the packaging is in tact. Make sure it has been kept at the right temperature. For ready cooked chicken or portions, check storage conditions, temperature and sell-by dates. Make sure it is properly sealed and the pack is undamaged.

Cream   Best bought from a reputable retailer with a fast turnover and reputation for fresh food as it goes off very quickly. The names and the way they are processed can be quite confusing – check the label, and if in doubt contact the manufacturer. There are two sources of infection, some harmful bacteria may remain if the milk has been inadequately pasteurised and once the cream is separated from the cooled milk it may become contaminated. This subsequent contamination is not likely if the cream has been subject to heat treatment a second time. If buying whipped cream check the label to see whether or not it contains stabilisers and sugar. Incidentally, aerosol cream has been heated by UHT and squirted into the cans in sterile conditions. The only minus is it tends to 'shrink' after squirting.

Cucumbers Do the 'shake and waggle test'. If it waves about, discard it. N.B. Use your common sense and don't wave the cucumber around too vigorously – even the top notch specimens will wobble if treated harshly. They should be firm to the touch and fresh smelling.

Duck If you buy a fresh chilled duck or duck recipe dish check for freshness, temperature and stick to reputable retailers with high quality standards and fast turnover.

Eggs As we saw earlier on, no one knows how many eggs are infected with salmonella – and indeed short of testing each egg, no one can tell. Since eggs are not marked with the producers name it has been very hard to track down infected hens. So play safe. Check the date of packing – if you don't understand the code – ask. Check the sell-by date, if there is one. Avoid eggs that have been stored near a sunny window or a radiator. Stick to reputable retailers who impose strict standards on their manufacturers and who have a high turnover of stock. Never buy cracked or dirty eggs.

Goats milk produce	Check for pasteurised milk or milk products that have been treated with UHT. Although the evidence to date on listeria suggests it is the type of cheese, rather than whether or not it has been pasteurised, which is crucial, you should always check when buying your cheese to see whether it was made from pasteurised milk, if you harbour the slightest doubts about these findings.
Lamb	Lamb should be fine grained and according to the experts, pinky-brown at the start of the season, dark pinky-brown later on. As with all meat and poultry, stick to reputable retailers who impose high standards on their suppliers and whose shops are run to rigorous standards of hygiene.
Leeks	Go for trimmed, well-shaped vegetables without any yellow or discoloured leaves. No-no's include: trimmed leeks which have their 'butt' (that's the small bulbous part above the root, to you and me) snipped. Once the butt has gone it seems, it is all downhill for the poor leek and it starts to deteriorate.
Lettuces	The humble lettuce can be harbouring listeria and in some cases pesticide residues. Make sure it is fresh, bright colour, no damaged or mouldy leaves. No-no's include: bruised leaves, slimy leaves, discolouration. Not always labelled clearly, so if in doubt about which

112

variety you are buying, ASK.

Milk We would advise you to play safe and stick to pasteurised milk. Avoid the so-called 'green top' which is raw, untreated milk. This type of milk cannot be sold in Scotland, where it was banned in August 1983. In England, Wales and Northern Ireland it can only be sold direct by the producer to the household consumer. The days of the milk bottle seem numbered, so when buying milk check the carton's sell-by date.

Offal Compared to our European neighbours, we British are not big on offal, that's liver, kidney, tripe, heart etc. Since the liver acts as a sort of toxic clearing house, those worried about pesticide residues are probably best to steer clear of it. For general comments, see beef, lamb.

Onions Stick to firm, dry onions with no sprouting or squidgy leaves. If buying salad onions, firmness is again a key quality. No-no's include: discoloured tops, sliminess.

Parsnips Tell-tale signs are: wizened specimens, brown patches, blemishes. Avoid these.

Pears These should be handled with care – by the retailer and by you – since pears are delicate things which bruise easily. You should buy when a wee bit unripe, i.e. firm-to-hard to the touch and ripen at home in the sun or, failing that, a warm

113

draught-free place.

Peas

It seems the humble pea was one of the earliest vegetables grown – they have even been found in stone age dwellings. That said, modern shoppers should look for bright green specimens. Wet pods or those with a greyish tinge spell disappointment and the likelihood of starchy, flavourless peas.

Pork

For general buying tips on pork, see our comments on beef and lamb. One key pointer with pork – colour does matter. The meat itself should be a delicate pale pink, gristle should be sparse and the fat firm and white.

Potatoes

PSST – PESTICIDE RESIDUE.
We know – the poor old potato has come in for a lot of stick in recent years. First, it was supposed to contribute to making us a nation of fatties and then no sooner was it rehabilitated with the fad of high fibre foods than a government report warns about high levels of pesticide residues in some potatoes. The problem lies in storing potatoes – and stopping them from continuing to grow. Our potatoes may be stored for up to ten months and to keep them in so-called 'mint' condition during this time they may be treated with chemicals, either to stop them sprouting or stop the growth of dangerous fungicides. Excessive residues from these growth retardants may prove harmful to

humans. Apart from that, what else should you look out for? No-no's include: damaged skins, diseased potatoes, signs of turning green, growth shoots. So-called 'new potatoes' are sent to the shops within hours of being dug up and should be eaten within a few days of purchase – but are one way of cutting down on the dreaded pesticide problem.

Raspberries   You need to play detective here. Avoid containers with stained bottoms – that could mean squashed fruit at the base. The fruit can go mouldy quickly, so stick to a fresh source of supply and make sure the fruit is not damp. Damp fruit is a perfect breeding ground for mould – and that's not something you want in either your kitchen or your tummy.

Salami   Avoid salami if not cured, it is raw meat and is likely to contain bacteria which may be poisonous.

Salmon   Salmon is once again growing in popularity – it was so common 100 years ago that servants even inserted a clause in their contract forbidding their employers to feed them salmon more than three times a week. If you are buying a whole salmon, look for bright eyes, red gill and a firm, resilient skin. If it is labelled 'do not refreeze', then you know it has already been frozen, make sure it is in good condition – and eat on day of purchase. Smoked salmon is raw fish which has been cured. The smoking and salting process kills bacteria but you should check the sell-by date and eating instructions.

Shrimps   Can be contaminated with bacteria and sometimes viruses. Poor processing may leave remains of these harmful bugs in the shrimp's gut. Always cook thoroughly and try to check country of origin.

Spinach   No-no's include: damaged leaves, dead foliage or signs of yellowing. Try to buy it freshly picked and eat within two days.

Strawberries See comments for raspberries above. If you buy mouldy strawberries, take back the whole box and complain. Don't just pick out the duds and forget about the problem.

Swedes   Stick to small and medium-sized specimens. No-no's include: damaged skins, signs of insects and overgrown swedes which have a woody flavour.

Sweetcorn   Best eaten on day of purchase. The so-called tassel, at the top of the cob should be brown and wispy. Take a quick peak at the cob itself if you can – it should be a sparkling sunshine yellow, with firm corn.

Tomatoes   PSST – PESTICIDES ABOUT.
Another favourite vegetable that surveys have shown tend to exhibit higher pesticide residues than many other less

popular 'fruit' (yes, it's technically a fruit). Choose your tomatoes with care. If you buy pallets of small or cherry tomatoes make sure they are all in good condition. Tomatoes are graded according to EEC standards, Extra and Class I being the best. If you are worried about pesticide residues, check your local retailer's policy on this matter.

Turkey   WATCH OUT – SALMONELLA ABOUT. Yes, we know all the fuss has focused on the poor old chicken – but many of the same hazards face the turkey too. What's more, we often make life more difficult for ourselves by reheating left over turkeys, buying extra large birds and then misjudging the cooking time, etc., etc. For general comments see chicken. No-no sign on frozen turkey: small, white, blistery spots – they could mean the bird has been stored for too long.

Turnips   Tell-tale signs to avoid: spongy texture, wormholes, over-large specimens, yellowish tinge, limpness.

Watercress One of those foods that 'granny' always warned against – since you could never be certain of the state of the water in which it was grown. Check for the code of practice symbol which should at least mean it left the producer in good shape – but also do your own inspection. Look for good colour, no yellowness, wilting, or stems

117

with too many side roots. Stick to retailers with a good reputation for fast turnover, food and store hygiene. Do NOT buy watercress unless you know it was grown in pure water.

Wheat
PSST – PESTICIDES ABOUT.
Well, now we have some good news and some bad news. The bad news first? OK. High pesticide residues may be found in wheat, particularly the bran. This is usually due to chemicals added during storage time. In addition, researchers from the Home Grown Cereals Authority reckon we may not be able to detect the true level of pesticides hiding away in our wheat as the chemicals bond with the cereals themselves and are not detected when using the standard analytical techniques for checking residues. Now, we are sure you are ready for the good news. Bread is one of the least likely foods to harbour harmful bacteria – it just does not provide the environment in which they thrive, and if you are worried about pesticides it seems rye bread is less likely to be contaminated than wheat.

Yogurt
Care is needed here. Yogurt is cultured milk with bacteria, yes, bacteria. As we have seen there are some bacteria which are 'goodies' as far as human beings are concerned and others which are the 'baddies'. Producers of yogurt need to be very careful to ensure they only cultivate the goodies, not the baddies. So please,

please be careful when you buy yogurt –
especially for children, the elderly or as a
healthy pick-up. Stick to well known
names from reputable retailers. Check
the date stamp – avoid battered cartons
or bloated containers. Check the
temperature it has been stored in. If
buying from fast food chain or market,
only do so if you are confident it has been
stored correctly.

Taking it home

If you buy fresh food, you should try to get it home as
quickly as possible. Don't buy it in the lunch hour and
leave it to warm up in the office. If you buy cook-chill
or frozen food take an insulated bag to carry the food
in. If you buy a large amount of frozen goods these are
sometimes placed in a box with dry ice to keep them
cold – be careful, this burns and should be handled
with care.

The moment you get home, wash your hands and then
sort out your shopping. Check your fridge temperature
(see next chapter) and put all fresh food in the
appropriate part of the fridge or freezer.

In the following chapter we will look at steps you can
take to reduce the risk of your home harbouring
infections.

CHAPTER SEVEN:
FOOD SAFETY IN THE HOME

A recent statement by Ross Buckland, President of the Food and Drink Federation, that poor hygiene by housewives was the prime cause of food poisoning, outraged many people. He claimed 60 per cent of poisonings happened in the home. Could this be right? Or was this just another example of industry passing the buck? Was Dr. Tim Lang, Director of the London Food Commission being fair when he responded, 'It is cheaper to blame the housewife than to overhaul the hygiene practices of an entire industry'. Or does the true picture lie somewhere in between?

Dangers in the kitchen

'Which' magazine conducted a survey into the health perils of our kitchens earlier this year which indicated that we do need to clean up our act. Out of 21 homes that their experts visited, only one was given a real pat on the back, the rest left a lot to be desired. Amongst the horrors they spotted were open rubbish bins, pets running freely on work surfaces, perished fridge seals, raw meat stored directly over cooked meat and fridges at the wrong temperatures.

But do we really care? It seems we do if the response

to the newly set up Food Safety Advisory Centre's Freephone service 'Foodline' is anything to go by. Sponsored by Asda, Gateway, Morrisons, Sainsbury's, Safeway and Tesco, its aim is to deal with questions the public may have about food safety. In addition, a pool of experts which include microbiologists, medical scientists, nutritionists and agricultural specialists, have been put together to give consumers the answers they seek and to contribute to the public debate on food safety matters. So what is it that is worrying us at the moment? We asked the Foodline experts in March to tell us what your top eight questions were in order of popularity. They were:

1) Home food storage such as fridge and freezer storage.

   Where and how to store food and at what temperatures? Also, is it safe to use cling film and tin foil?

2) Salmonella

   How safe are eggs? Which egg dishes are the least risky? Also about poultry, how should it be cooked safely?

3) Listeria

   Which soft cheeses are not regarded as safe? On cook-chill meals, you wondered how you could tell that it was thoroughly heated?

4) Home hygiene

   How can we avoid food poisoning at home?

5) Supermarkets

   Queries including what do 'sell-by' and 'eat-by' dates mean? Where dried or frozen egg could be obtained and what happens when supermarkets recall products?

6) About bacteria, BSE the cattle disease and BST (administered to cattle to improve milk yield), and pasteurization of milk, yoghurt and dairy products?

7) General questions about cooking methods.

   You asked about microwave usage, pressure cooker and slow cooker. Also, about the usage of aluminium pans and foil.

8) Health and technical questions.

   You asked about aluminium levels in soya milk, the residue of dioxins in nappies etc, and possible alternative products and the question of pesticide usages and residue levels in foods.

So there is no doubt we are more aware of problems and better informed about the risks in the food we eat. But whilst the food industry needs to take urgent action to rid our food of unacceptable levels of contamination, their efforts will be a total waste of time if we allow bad hygiene practices in the home to re-contaminate our food. So we, as individual consumers, must play our part in protecting ourselves.

Bug busters

Most of the scientists we spoke to, such as Dr. Verner Wheelock and Dr. Robert Park, felt that if we knew more about food hygiene and the facts about the bugs that may be in our food then the present escalating food poisoning trends could be reversed. Dr. Park, a senior lecturer in Microbiology at Reading University, explained that in order to beat the harmful bacteria, we need to know a little about their life-cycle. The first thing we need to understand is that bacteria can only flourish if five essential conditions exist. These are:

- Sufficient food. Much of the protein we eat, the bacteria like as well.

- Favourable temperature. Most bacteria really multiply fast at 98.6°, although some bacteria such as listeria can multiply at temperatures down to 0°C.

- Enough time. The longer they have, the more they multiply.

- Available moisture. In dry conditions, bacteria won't grow.

- The right atmosphere. Some bacteria grow with air and some without.

Remove any one of these conditions and you can win the battle of the bugs. The second thing we need to understand is that food-related illness can be divided into two categories:

- Food poisoning
  The food actually plays a part by allowing the organisms to grow in it, producing poisons, known as toxins. So the food is actually already either poisonous when we eat it or potentially poisonous, since it produces toxins in the gut. We can beat this

type of illness by refrigerating, freezing or making our food acidic or dry.

- Food borne infection

The bacteria or organism uses the food as a vehicle and gets carried to us in agents such as water, milk and foodstuffs. The bugs generally need to be present in large numbers of living cells if they are to cause illness. Refrigeration will not make any difference to these organisms, but cooking properly will and so will care over hygiene when we are preparing the food.

So as you can see, we can actively cut food poisoning risks at home with a little 'science appliance'. The main risk areas are outlined in the Food and Drink Federation's leaflet 'Common Sense about Foodcare in the Kitchen'. These are:

- Cross contamination between raw and cooked food.

- Insufficient thawing of frozen poultry.

- Undercooking food, especially meat and poultry.

- Cooling cooked foods too slowly before refrigeration.

- Preparing food too far in advance.

- Storing food in a warm place.

- Not reheating food to a high enough temperature to kill food poisoning bacteria and destroy toxins.

Food safety tips

The following list of food safety tips has been compiled with the help of environmental health officers, home economists and a microbiologist.

Kitchen design

Ensure that where different surfaces join, there are no gaps where food and dirt can become trapped. Gaps in the grouting between tiles can cause a problem as well, so fill any gaps with a suitable sealant.

Work surfaces

Harmful bacteria seek sanctuary in dirt and grease so regular cleaning and scrubbing will cut down the risk of tiny scraps of food cross-infecting the food that you are preparing. Better to clean work tops each time they are used rather than once a week.

Rubber gloves

They're not just for keeping your hands smooth and soft! They allow you to wash-up in water that is hotter than your hands can normally bear. It is advisable to keep one pair for food preparation and washing up and another pair for dirty jobs such as laundry, cleaning the toilet and the bathroom.

Chopping boards

The old-fashioned wooden chopping board is fine for cutting bread, but if it becomes scored and damaged it is a potential trap for bacteria. So for cutting meat it is wise to invest in a synthetic polyblock type of board which can be soaked and sterilised. Remember to wash the board between cutting up different types of meat.

Teatowels
If you can drain and air dry your washing up you are less likely to put bacteria onto your dishes from your teatowel. If you do use a teatowel make sure that it is changed often (daily if possible). Don't forget the oven glove either, the same rule applies.

Dishcloths
Sterilise with bleach, disinfectant or by boiling for five minutes regularly, and store dry.

Kitchen towel
The advantage of this method of cleaning and wiping is that bacteria are thrown away with the towel. Always try and use a paper towel if wiping up meat juices.

Kitchen utensils
This tip was given to us by Dr Joseph Selkon, Director of Public Health, Oxfordshire Regional Public Health Laboratory at the John Radcliffe Hospital. Use separate utensils for cutting raw and cooked meats and separate boards. You could keep these separate by buying knives with different coloured handles, say red for raw and blue for cooked meats. Simple, but he reckons that this above all other precautions would cut down home poisoning incidents. Also, pay special

attention to cleaning such things as food processors, mixers, mincers and graters to ensure that all tiny pieces of food are removed. Wooden spoons that are porous and easily damaged can harbour bugs so dispose of any that are cracked or damaged.

Bins

Small bins are better than larger ones because you have to empty them more often, not allowing bacteria time to breed. Lids are essential to keep vermin, pets and flies off your rubbish. Clean out regularly with disinfectant, paying special attention to the underside of the lid. Outdoor dustbins need regular cleaning as well and if you use those heavy duty plastic dustbin bags try not to leave them where our canine and feline friends can get at them and spread the contents over the garden or pavement.

Pets

Train your cat (yes, you can!) not to jump up and walk over surfaces, especially in the kitchen. Use separate utensils and dishes for petfood and don't let them lick scraps off your plates. Accidents will happen, so if your pet messes indoors remove the worst of it with newspaper or kitchen towel, which you can put directly into the dustbin or incinerator. Then thoroughly disinfect the affected area and your hands as well. However much you love your pet avoid kissing it, remember how they wash themselves and where! Always wash your hands between stroking your pet and handling food.

Vermin

Rats make most people shudder, but mice have equally disgusting social habits. Our houses act as nursery, cafeteria and toilet and the evidence is usually dropped in cupboards and drawers. If you decide to eradicate these unwelcome visitors by using the spring-loaded trap, remember when baiting them, that mice are not, contrary to popular opinion, crazy about cheese. They much prefer nuts, raisins, oats or if you are feeling generous a nice piece of chocolate. If you are thinking of using poison remember that some mice have become resistant to Warfarin, so seek professional advice from your local environmental health department.

Creepy crawlies

Flies love garbage, the more decomposed the better, and that's not all they put their feet in. Don't leave food out where they can get at it unless you're fond of maggots. Keep your kitchen a fly-free zone but remember if using a flyspray, to cover food and to wipe any fallout off surfaces and worktops. Ants and cockroaches spread bacteria as well, so do not encourage them to visit by leaving tempting morsels around. If things get out of hand call the experts in, that's what they are there for.

129

Toilets	Disinfect frequently, allow the lavatory brush to air-dry after use. Always wash hands afterwards.
Cooking preparation	Wash all vegetables, fruit and salads. Thoroughly defrost any meat or poultry to be cooked. Check use-by dates on processed foods. Remember, because of today's trends towards healthier eating, foods marked additive or preservative free will have a correspondingly shorter shelf life than foods containing those added chemicals.
Home water filtration units	If you have fitted one of these in your home it's effectiveness is only as good as the maintenance you give it. Environmental health officers we spoke to were concerned that some people may be getting water-borne illnesses as a result of not changing filters in accordance with the manufacturer's instructions. Old filters can become a reservoir for bacteria, especially if other recommended treatment is ignored.

Safe storage

We can help to conquer the bugs if we store our food safely. Here we give you some tips:

Refrigerator

1) Keep temperature between 1°C (34°F) and 5°C (41°F).

2) Buy a large enough fridge as overloading it stops the circulation of cold air.

3) Keep your fridge defrosted. If you grow titanic size icebergs in your freezer compartment then the fridge will work inefficiently. Remember it is cooler at the bottom.

4) Clean it out regularly paying special attention to the door seals, racking and any spillages. A weak solution of Bi-carbonate of Soda in warm water is recommended. This also means you can inspect your stored food for signs of decomposition and dispose of any growing fur jackets of mould or 'passed its use by date'.

5) Always store cooked meats above raw meats.

6) Cover foods tightly with cling film (if you are worried about using cling film check manufacturers' guidance on the packaging), tin foil or place in air tight containers.

7) Do not put warm food directly into the fridge. A quick way of cooling food down is to put it in an air-tight container and stand it in cold water till it cools.

8) Buy a fridge thermometer, do not guess the temperature. They are cheap and show you that your fridge is working efficiently. It should be operating at between 1°C and 5°C (34°F and 41°F).

Freezer

1) Keep below 18°C (0°F).

2) Freezing food does not kill bacteria but it does stop them growing. Contaminated food will remain that way – so always freeze food that is fresh or freshly cooked and wholesome.

3) Do not let some long forgotten meal become a mystery package – label and date frozen food. Remember even frozen food has a recommended storage life, i.e. beef and chicken 12 months, white fish 4 months, smoked bacon 2 months, hard cheese 3 months, baked goods 3 months and sausages 1 month. Why not add your own use by date to the label?

4) Never re-freeze food that has been thawed out unless you cook it well in between.

5) If you buy commercially frozen food follow recommended keeping times.
   * 1 Week ** 1 Month *** for 3 months, – for home freezing your freezer should have the **** symbol.

6) Remember thawing food out in a warm environment over a long period of time will give bacteria time to grow and increase – so avoid this practice.

7) Deep freezers should be kept at a temperature of 18°C (0°F) and you can use a freezer thermometer to check that the temperature is correct.

Temperatures at which most bacteria grow and die

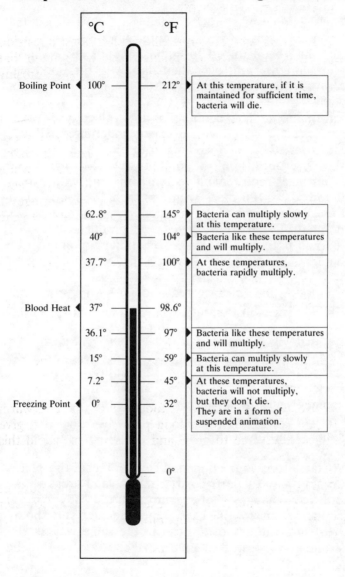

Boiling Point ◀ 100° —— 212° | At this temperature, if it is maintained for sufficient time, bacteria will die.

62.8° —— 145° | Bacteria can multiply slowly at this temperature.

40° —— 104° | Bacteria like these temperatures and will multiply.

37.7° —— 100° | At these temperatures, bacteria rapidly multiply.

Blood Heat ◀ 37° —— 98.6°

36.1° —— 97° | Bacteria like these temperatures and will multiply.

15° —— 59° | Bacteria can multiply slowly at this temperature.

7.2° —— 45° | At these temperatures, bacteria will not multiply, but they don't die. They are in a form of suspended animation.

Freezing Point ◀ 0° —— 32°

0°

Canned goods

On the topic of storing canned goods, we called the Canned Goods Advisory service only to discover that they had been forced to withdraw their advice sheet after disagreement over their data with the Food and Drink Federation. However, the technical division of Asda came to our rescue with the following information: 'The canning of a product gives us a sterile/safe product, with an almost indefinite shelf life. However, there is a slow deterioration of quality and flavours. Because of the long possible shelf life, there is no legal requirement to mark the can with a best before date.' Products with less than 18 months shelf life are required to be marked however and as we pointed out earlier we believe all products should be marked both with the date of manufacture and eat by date.

The following are suggested guidelines for storing your canned goods at home:

Canned vegetables	12 months
Canned fruit	12 months
Caned fish	12 months
Caned meats	9 months
Canned sauces/ready meals	9 months
Canned dairy products	6 months
Canned carbonate drinks	6 months

Always store your unopened cans in a cool dry place. Avoid damp or partially damp areas and areas where drastic changes of temperature may cause condensation on the cans. Once opened you should treat the contents of the can in the same way as you would treat fresh food. Do not keep the food in the can but empty the contents into a container and keep in a refrigerator for a maximum of two days.

Dried foods

Thanks to Asda again for this information. All dried goods rely on their low water content for their length of life. If they get damp they will spoil rapidly. The following advice for the storage of dried foods at home is given in the absence of any manufacturer's recommendations that might be quoted on the packaging.

Pasta	12 months
Rice	12 months
Pulses	12 months
Dried fruits	6 months if not date coded
Plain flour	12 months if not date coded
S.R. flour	6 months if not date coded

Always store your dried food in a cool, dry place. Avoid damp areas or damp cupboards, for example, above a steaming kettle. Remember to use airtight containers if you can, once opened. If you use up half packets don't lose them at the back of your cupboard. Be careful not to let your open packets attract mice. Why not mark your own stored goods with a use by date? All you need is a felt tip pen.

Microwave cooking

1) The microwave's reputation has taken a bit of a battering recently especially where listeria is concerned. The golden rule is 'use it according to

the manufacturer's instructions'. If you do not have a handbook then send off for one. The power of the microwave can range between 400 and 700 watts, the lower the wattage the longer the cooking time will be.

2) Do not overload your microwave – too much food or too large a piece will mean cold spots if cooked for insufficient time.

3) If cooking casseroles or foods in liquid stir during cooking to distribute heat throughout.

4) Cover liquid food to avoid food spattering over the microwave.

5) When using cling film check the instructions on the box, some films are suitable for cooking others are not.

6) Always allow the recommended standing time as this is part of the cooking process.

Personal hygiene

1) Wash hands before and in between touching foodstuffs, stroking your pet, handling rubbish, using the toilet.

2) Avoid touching your mouth and nose whilst preparing food and also do not smoke as your hands would come into contact with your mouth. Also do not cough or sneeze over food.

3) Cover all wounds or sores with waterproof plasters – do not handle food if your stomach is upset.

Entertaining

1) Take care to properly refrigerate any food cooked in advance and do not cook too far in advance.

2) Ensure at barbecues that meat is thoroughly cooked, especially chicken. Keep meats apart and in the fridge until you need them.

3) Remember the rule 'if in doubt, throw it out', especially if entertaining.

4) Leftovers should be refrigerated or frozen as quickly as possible, not after several hours when your guests have left.

Eating out

1) Do not be frightened to complain if you think something is wrong either with the food or the hygiene standards. Remember things will probably only improve if you keep complaining.

2) Your local environmental health department *does* want to hear from you if you or your party fall ill. It helps them to follow up such cases.

3) Be 'pickey' if you fancy a takeaway, far better if you can see your food actually being cooked and that the premises and food handlers are spotless. Grubby looking people probably pay the same sort of attention to the food they sell.

4) You can always ask to see the kitchens, if you are in any doubt.

On holiday

1) If abroad, play safe, do not drink the tap water, used bottled water for drinking, cleaning your teeth, and remember ice cubes are often made with ordinary water.

2) Avoid ice cream vendors if overseas.

3) Remember many beaches at home and abroad are contaminated with raw stewage, so picnics on the beach are inadvisable. Wash or shower thoroughly after leaving the beach.

CHAPTER EIGHT:
ACTION PLANS FOR AT RISK GROUPS

In the midst of all this food hysteria, it is easy to adopt either a neurotic attitude and worry incessantly about everything you eat or to become complacent and say 'it does not affect me, I've been eating the same type of food for years with no harmful effects'. Neither of these extreme attitudes is correct. What we need to do is cooly assess the facts – once we have them at our fingertips. This is what we have tried to do so far in this book.

At risk groups

So who is at risk? First of all, let's look at bacterial infections. You may well have heard that those at risk are groups who are 'immune suppressed'. What, you may well wonder, does that term mean? Can we in fact tell who is likely to get sick? The following case study shows how 'selective' the bugs may be.

A group of university students decided to celebrate the end of term with an al fresco picnic. Shopping for the party was done the previous day. It included bread, butter, a large wadge of pâté and, of course, the occasional bottle of plonk. The day of the picnic dawned, warm and sunny, the hamper was packed and the party set off to hire some punts for the day. There were 28 people and because their destination was a grassy bank some miles away and owing to their ineptitude with the punt poles it took some hours to get there. As a result they ate lunch in late afternoon. Later that day 19 students were struck down with food poisoning, which subsequently turned out to be staphylococcus. But what about the nine students who were unaffected? They all ate the pâté, which proved to be responsible, so why did they not get sick?

There appear to be two factors that can be used to identify those who are particularly vulnerable, according to Dr L Poulter, senior lecturer from the Department of Immunology at the Royal Free Hospital School of Medicine. The first are those people who have a suppressed or compromised immune system, that is those whose natural defences against disease are run down. The second are those people who because of their genes are unable to recognise and kill certain organisms. The following types of people could be considered 'at risk'.

1) *Babies and toddlers* – up to three years of age. By the time children reach five years old their immune systems should be fully formed and functioning.

2) *Expectant mothers* – The foetus is more likely to be at risk than the mother, although her immune system is likely to be somewhat suppressed in order to stop her body rejecting the foetus.

3) *Older people* – This group may already have weakened immune systems from fighting off other diseases or they might be part of the next category.

140

4) *Socially deprived people* – There is very good evidence that social deprivation predisposes people to infection. If you think back fifty to a hundred years ago the treatment for tuberculosis, before penicillin became widely available, was simply to move people to a better and cleaner environment where they would recover. Those left behind in cramped conditions, poor social and economical situations did not recover. People today who face those sort of conditions are more likely to be predisposed to illness in general.

5) *People who are immuno suppressed for clinical reasons* – Such as patients who have undergone transplants or those who are on long term corticosteroids for whatever reasons.

6) *Aids sufferers and certain types of cancer patients, such as sufferers from leukaemia.*

7) *Travellers* – This group could be susceptible because they might visit an environment with organisms that were new to them and which their immune system would have no 'memory' of.

8) *Long term sufferers of stress related illnesses* – There seems to be a certain connection between neurophysiology and the immune system. Evidence exists that protracted sufferers of stress show more susceptibility to say, a flu epidemic, so it is logical to conclude they might be susceptible to increased cases of food poisoning as well. No doubt this is a case for future research.

And finally, if you don't appear on this list, sadly you may still have a chance of suffering one of our countries most frequent illnesses! If you are unlucky enough to eat contaminated food and the number of organisms present is sufficiently high, then you could simply overload your immune system and get sick.

Action plans for at risk groups

Infants and toddlers: One of the greatest risk factors with an infant is gastro-enteritis, which can, if not treated promptly, lead to dehydration, debility and death. To cut down the risk of infection or cross-infection, attention to hygiene is of paramount importance. Scrupulous cleaning of feeding equipment, be it breast or bottle, is essential. Before breast feeding wash your hands well. Be careful not to initiate cross-infection by allowing hands soiled by dirty nappies to come into contact with your baby's mouth. Also, do not touch your own nose or mouth whilst feeding. Bottles should be carefully disinfected. Rinse with cold water first, teats should then be turned inside out and boiled together with the bottle for two minutes. Alternately, use a Hypochlorite solution at recommended strengths. Ensure teats are totally submerged. Also, take care to wash hands after touching a pet.

Toddlers will have a certain degree of acquired immunity but care must still be taken. Ensure that everything your toddler eats is thoroughly cooked and that you never handle raw and cooked meats at the same time without washing your hands in between. The same rule applies to knives, chopping boards, food processors and mincers.

Toilet training should include teaching your child to

wash hands immediately afterwards, also before meals and after handling a pet. Special attention to kitchen hygiene will help. Always cover cuts, refrigerate all pre-cooked food as quickly as you can, keep flies off food and last but not least do not mix old foods to new when making up your toddler's meals.

Expectant mums: Sir Donald Acheson, the Chief Medical Officer, recently issued a health warning to all pregnant women with reference to listeria. The message was, 'avoid eating soft ripened cheeses such as Brie, Camembert and blue vein types. There is also a small risk from ready-to-eat cooked poultry and cook-chill meals and it would be prudent for pregnant women to re-heat these types of food till they are piping hot. Always ensure that microwaved food is cooked throughout with no 'cold spots' and allow the recommended standing time.'

Ian McFadyen, the Royal College of Obstetricians and Gynaecologists' representative to the Department of Health, stressed the need to reduce caffeine intake. Since caffeine is present in coffee, cola, chocolate and many other foods he says it is impossible to cut out altogether. His message is 'cut it down'. He said pregnant mothers should use their common sense about diet. If they are vegetarians, they may well need to take vitamin supplements in order to make sure not only that they are healthy but that their baby in turn is healthy. According to Mr McFadyen, some Britons who have turned vegetarian may well be short of folic acid – which is vital for the baby's normal development and they may need to take supplements not only through pregnancy but during breast feeding as well. Discuss the matter with your GP.

If you plan to travel abroad, be careful there may be bugs around which your system is not geared up to destroy. Toxoplasmosis, a parasite, can cause severe foetal complications. Therefore expectant mums are advised to avoid eating undercooked meat in any form. If in doubt consult with your local GP or antenatal clinic.

If you become pregnant and are using any medication or plan to take some, check with your doctor as certain drugs may have different side effects once you are expecting.

Older people: If you are fit and healthy and follow the healthy eating and hygiene guidance in this book, then there should be no problems. If however you have been ill recently, are recovering from surgery or are caring for a sick friend or relative, then extra precautions should be taken which include: storing foods in the refrigerator, not cooking food too much in advance, extra vigilance in personal hygiene, keeping cooked and uncooked foods separate at all times, throwing away left-over re-heated foods, and always store cooked foods over uncooked foods in the fridge.

Socially disadvantaged: Make sure that you are receiving all the benefits you are entitled to. Try to follow the tips for healthier eating for the other at risk groups, remember many harmful bacteria are killed by exposure to sufficient heat and food left around at room temperature for a sufficient length of time has more chance of being contaminated.

Immuno suppressed and AIDS patients: The Chief Medical Officer, Sir Donald Acheson advises all immunocompromised patients, transplant recipients, patients with leukaemias and lymphoid malignancies and those on immuno-suppressive drugs including oral and systemic steroids to follow the same advice given to pregnant women.

Travellers: Correct vaccinations for area of travel as advised by your G.P. Take care to eat well cooked foods and drink sterilised or bottled water. Remember the native population will have an acquired immunity to their bugs, you probably won't.

Bug recognition

Remember that our bodies are designed to fight bacteria and they need to be kept alert. If we managed to kill all the harmful bacteria in our environment, then we would not be in a position to fight the bacteria when we came into contact with them. As Dr Poulter stated in his article in this year's issue of the industries' own magazine, *Food Production*: 'It is important to realise at the outset, that the entry of thousands of microbes, into our body occurs quite naturally every day, yet we are not constantly ill. The reason for this is that our body is designed to thrive in the natural environment we live in. An important part of that design is our immune defence system. This is an intricate network of mechanisms that are spread throughout the body. Cells of our immune system survey our tissue constantly, like sentries on guard, to prevent any invasion by microbes. This surveillance system is further capable of storing a memory of any microbe it sees, so that it will be recognised rapidly, should it reappear, when powerful mechanisms to eliminate the infection will be switched on. We make use of this memory when we vaccinate our children against whooping cough, polio or measles.'

Chemical attack

While our bodies are designed to fight bacteria, they are not arguably designed to fight the cocktail of chemicals we are eating, drinking and breathing. As Dr Poulter confirmed: 'on the question of pesticides it is a much more serious issue . . . it is quite possible that there are chemicals within pesticides that we are not equipped to deal with – in the sense that they would be toxic to the point where our immune system would not be effective.' In other words when it comes to chemicals the at risk group includes *us all*.

The problem with trying to assess the impact of chemicals on our system is seemingly insurmoutable. As Dr Poulter said: 'the problem is that we just do not know what is dangerous, what is a good level and what is a bad level. I cannot envisage a way, short of selecting 2,000 people and running experiments on them, how you could find out. Even then you would have to run experiments for many years because some of these things are cumulative.' All we can do is try to reduce the amount of pesticides we eat (see p. 88) and put pressure on the authorities to take *urgent* steps to minimise pesticide residues and other chemicals in our food and water.

We know the symptoms and likely duration of food poisoning as a result of harmful bacteria – but it may be years, even generations, before we know the effects of eating food stuffed with chemicals. The chemical timebomb we referred to in chapter five is ticking away . . .

146

CHAPTER NINE:
WHAT TO DO IF THE BUGS STRIKE

Listeria hysteria?

Amanda Jupp and her husband Tim were looking forward to the birth of their first child who was due at the end of August 1987. Then about five weeks before her baby was due, Amanda was taken ill with what she thought was flu. Her doctor agreed, as she was displaying all the symptoms, aching limbs, hot and cold sweats and headaches. She was ill for the next fortnight and then somewhat unexpectedly went into labour just over three weeks prematurely. What started off as a normal labour turned into an emergency when it was discovered that her baby was becoming severely distressed, and preparations were made to perform a caesarean section. In the event, it proved to be unnecessary as she was able to give birth normally after eight hours of being in labour.

Matthew came into the world on the 3rd August 1987 but instead of a hearty yell, he was totally silent. In fact he didn't respond to anything, his eyes remained closed and he didn't move at all. His blood sugar was discovered to be abnormally high and his heart rate was erratic. This was put down to the results of a stressful labour but that did not account for his high temperature. It soon became obvious to the medical staff that his condition was abnormal. He appeared to be in a deep, totally unconscious sleep, and after some hours he developed a measles-like rash. At that point he was transferred to the Special Care Baby Unit for tests and by this time he was having trouble breathing. At the same time Amanda was taken to an isolation ward.

After a while Amanda was asked to call her husband as their baby was deteriorating fast, indeed he was not expected to survive. The cause was still a mystery and in their hunt for clues, the doctors took samples of Amanda's body fluids, as they suspected whatever Matthew had, his mother had given him. A little while later the results came back, Amanda's birth canal was riddled with listeria and bacteria were found to be in Matthew's spinal fluid. The Jupps were beside themselves with worry, neither of them had ever heard of listeria. Their son was barely alive 24 hours after his birth, surviving in an incubator with the help of a ventilator. To make matters worse every so often his little body would leap uncontrollably as the result of massive spasms and the fits he was having. There were two facts in his favour however. One was that he was born almost full term and weighed 6 lbs 7 oz at birth which probably saved his life, the other was the expertise of the medical team, who did have a little experience of listeriosis and were able to treat him with the right antibiotics, without which he would certainly have had brain damage or worse. Matthew survived and is now coming up to his second birthday, but Amanda still blames herself for giving her son listeriosis. But how could she have known?

After all Sir Donald Acheson only wrote to 'all doctors in England' with his warnings to expectant mothers on the 16th February 1989. And a year or so before George Pinker, President of the Royal College of Obstetricians and Gynaecologists was sounding warnings to his colleagues. In 1986 the London Food Commission reported its findings on listeria to the Department of Health and when we checked in the fifth edition of the book 'Food Poisoning and Food Hygiene' by Betty Hobbs and Diane Roberts, it clearly states that there was an outbreak of listeriosis in 1985 which involved 58 Mother and Infant pairs and that was two years before Matthew was conceived! So why did it take the government so long to warn the public? Just a few simple words of advice could have saved the Jupp family from a nightmare experience. The fact that listeria is a rare illness is irrelevant to Amanda Jupp and to Matthew.

Coffee, tea or staphylococcus aureus?

Ann and Martin Hart decided to have a six-day break in Egypt. When they arrived at the start of their holiday, they were well aware of the risk of 'Cairo Tummy', so took extra special care to drink bottled water and eat safe, well-cooked food. Ann remembers on the return flight that the cold lunches, which consisted of cold chicken and salad were in fact lukewarm. She put this down to the fact that the flight was delayed, temperature at Cairo Airport was around 101°F and the food container was left out on the tarmac.

In the event she was probably right, as she remembers rejecting something because it didn't look too good and the following day both she and Martin suffered agonising stomach cramps followed by severe bouts of diarrhoea. Her doctor sent some stool samples to be tested and staphylococcus aureus was found to be the culprit. They did not complain to the airline at the time because they both thought the blame would be put on food they had eaten on holiday but subsequently they discovered other passengers on the same flight had also been ill.

The moral of this story is that just one slip in the hygiene chain can cause many people to suffer and caterers should be vigilant to see this does not happen. But how could they know that it did, if no one complained?

Dr Verner Wheelock, head of the food policy research unit at Bradford University has this advice for people who suspect they have been made ill as a result of food poisoning. If people don't report, how can standards be improved? They will, if business is lost due to poor hygiene, but they do need to know when and how. Avoid pointing the accusing finger at a specific foodstuff unless you have laboratory evidence. Complain in writing to the caterers (keeping a copy) and also to your local environmental health officer.

The 'crypto' factor 89

Crytosporidium is a nasty bug, as people in the Oxford and Swindon area found out. It is a tiny parasite, present in animals and first recognised as an agent of infection in humans in 1976. Thanks to the vigilance of Dr Richardson, registrar at the Princess Margaret Hospital in Swindon and Microbiologist Dr Bucks, increased cases of profuse diarrhoea began to ring alarm bells. That was back in January and by February they were plotting the incidences on a map and using plenty of pins, reflecting the substantial rise in the number of cases. Between the 2nd January and the 20th February there were 55 reported cases compared with 48 for the whole of the previous year.

At the same time the increase of laboratory diagnosis was noticed by the Oxford Public Health Laboratory. Dr Mayon-White, Community Physician for the Oxfordshire District Health Authority obtained information from The Communicable Diseases Surveillance Centre about the increase in cases in the Swindon Area. Oxford's Department of Community Medicine started to investigate into possible causes but could find no common factor.

Back in Swindon, Dr Richardson's map provided a vital clue. The sufferers all came from an area that received their water supply from the Farmoor Reservoir belonging to the Thames Water Authority. The authority was tipped off on 14th February, initially, and on 17th February they accepted that there was sufficient evidence to warrant immediate action. Whilst the scientist got to work to test water samples from Farmoor, Thames Water put out an official 'Red Alert'.

No public statement was made until the results of laboratory testing were available. They proved positive, with large numbers of cryptosoridia in filters and backwash areas. An urgent meeting was organised by the Oxford and Swindon Health Authorities on Monday 20th February 1989, to arrive at a policy decision on how to handle the epidemic. At 6 p.m. that same evening a press statement was released to the media and simultaneously both the Water Authority and the two District Health Authorities set up a 24 hour phone line to cope with customer enquiries. Some customers felt that Thames Water should have been more aware of the possibility of a cryptosporidiosis outbreak. Some disbelief was expressed that a test method had to be devised and instituted so quickly when there had been testing for cryptosporidia for some years.

(The above information was taken from the Report of an Inquiry into Water Supplies in Oxford and Swindon following an outbreak of Cryptosporidiosis during February-March 1989.)

For many years now we have had confidence in British water. Turn on the tap and watch the flow of clear, clean water. Clean as the image of the water authorities, who treat, filter and test this basic commodity. But for one family that image was sorely dented when little Jamie Thurley, at the tender age of sixteen months, developed diarrhoea on Tuesday 16th February 1989. By the Friday his parents Denis and Karen were worried enough to take him to their doctor. As he had a sniffle and diarrhoea the doctor assumed that he was treating a cold and advised Karen to give the baby plenty of fluids, which in this case was orange squash and, of course, tap water.

On the 20th February Karen caught something on the radio about a problem with water, so she called Thames Water to find out if they were in the affected area. They confirmed that Highworth was and advised her that she should boil tap water for one minute to lessen the risk of cryptosporidosis. This advice however was too late, baby Jamie was worse, to add to the diarrhoea he was suffering from stomach pains that were so severe that he cried for up to four hours continuously and no amount of consoling by his parents could ease his suffering. His G.P. had sent a sample of faeces off to the laboratory and the results confirmed cryptosporidosis.

In the meantime five other members of the Thurley family had gone down with stomach cramps and diarrhoea. They however recovered after a few days, unlike Jamie. Two weeks later, by which time he was, as his father put it, skin and bones, another laboratory test indicated heavy infestation of the cryptosporia parasite and another organism giardia. Giardia, according to a letter issued by the Pool Water Treatment Advisory Group in January 1989, has 'traditionally been an issue for drinking water treatment'. So Jamie was suffering from two, possibly water borne, organisms. Eventual antibiotic treatment restored the baby to good health after a month of suffering but his father, Denis, was understandably angry about what happened. He has registered, along with some 200 other people with the Swindon victims group, based at a local Citizen's Advice Bureau. They held a number of public meetings to discuss the whole issue. Thames Water's representative found himself being shouted down when he attempted to reassure those present that the number of reported cases were indeed falling. Of course they were falling, since most people weren't drinking the water anyway the audience responded!

Thames Water took further measures to dampen public alarm when they issued a letter to their customers on the 31st March, the gist of which was:

'Dear Customer,
As you will be aware, from the middle of February,

153

there was an increase in the incidence of diarrhoea caused by cryptosporidia in parts of Oxfordshire and the Swindon area. Because of the possible link between this outbreak and the water supply from our Farmoor works, we took the precaution of advising that drinking water for children under the age of two, should be boiled for one minute. This advice was also given to those individuals who's immune systems were not operating normally. We have recently been reassured by the local health authorities, that the number of cases of illness caused by the organism has reduced to the level, which is normal, and results from the presence of cryptosporidia in the environment. We have therefore been able to announce that the precautionary advice that had previously been given – is no longer necessary. We apologise for the inconvenience that these precautions have caused some of our customers. We believe, however, that the actions we took and the advice we gave our customers, were sensible precautions, reflecting the fact that the health of our customers was our highest priority.'

Denis and Karen Thurley, however, are still boiling their drinking water.

We spoke to Dr. Mayon-White to find out how such incidents are reported. In the formal notification system certain diseases are designated notifiable and these include food poisoning and interestingly, suspected food poisoning. The doctor or G.P. is obliged to report these notifiable diseases (although we gather no doctor has ever been prosecuted for not doing so), to the community physician or someone who has been designated medical officer for environmental health. These notices arrive by post and they are then reported each week to the Office of Population, Census and Surveys. On a local level the community physician or medical officer keeps his eyes open for any abnormal number of outbreaks that might indicate trouble in the environment. At the same time environmental health officers and the laboratories also submit reports. Outbreaks are usually dealt with on a local level.

Dr Mayon-White would like to see better communication at all levels and with the wisdom of hindsight he feels that someone should be designated to be in overall charge of such incidents, where so many different people are involved.

We ask:

Are the reporting systems adequate and is there sufficient liaison between the different bodies?

Is it right that people actually have to become sick before authorities are alerted to problems?

Should those responsible for pollution be held legally liable to compensate those made ill by their negligence?

At a time when one in three of Britain's farming and food scientists face unemployment and many food safety projects are likely to be cut because of lack of government funding, should we be lobbying to reverse these cuts?

We feel the public have the right to information, all information that might affect their health or the health of their children, so that informed choice might be made.

Salmonella Sunday

April Walton remembers that day only too well. It was during the middle of the salmonella in eggs scare. Edwina Curry was saying one thing, the farmers another and the government it seemed said very little. But April was not taking any chance with her family, eggs were out, until the situation became clearer.

The family were looking forward to the weekend as they had been invited to join the local group of conservation volunteers who were working on a project restoring an ancient barn. Saturday went well but on Sunday, the weather was at its worst. In fact it was so bad that the Walton family decided to stay at home. April was not expecting to have to cook lunch, so she did what she always did at a time like this, raided her deep freeze. The chicken she got out went into a bowl of warm water for rapid defrosting. Her family enjoyed the hurriedly prepared meal of roast chicken with all the trimmings and settled down that afternoon to watch the television.

It was in the middle of the night that April was woken up by her seven year old son, Robert. He was shivering and said that he felt sick. Within the next hour, both he and April were suffering from bouts of severe diarrhoea. April's husband Tony spent most of that night looking after them and was on the phone at 8.30 a.m. the following morning to call out their G.P. By the time he arrived, Robert was in a state of collapse and suffering from extreme dehydration, so their doctor decided to have him admitted to the local hospital.

At the hospital a sample of Robert's faeces was sent to

the laboratory for testing and after three days, salmonella enteritidis was diagnosed. Tony had the presence of mind to retrieve some of the chicken from the kitchen bin, and that subsequently, upon testing, proved to be the culprit. It took well over a week for April and Robert to recover and left April feeling angry at the government for coming to the aid of the poultry farmers so readily during the salmonella row. Why was it that she was buying food that was already contaminated? Surely after her experience, chickens should carry a 'Government Health Warning'.

- We believe all consumers should press for greater access to information with regards to food standards.

- Positive action should be taken by the agriculture industry in view of the fact that up to six out of ten chickens may be contaminated in varying degrees with salmonella.

- The public should have access to the communicable disease reports that are issued weekly and reflect the latest statisics from across the country, in order that consumers make informed choices when buying food.

Coping with food poisoning

In this section we look at the main bugs which might lay you low. We explain the symptoms, tell you how long you are likely to be ill, the treatment you can expect and equally important, how to beat the bugs in the first place. We have started the list with the more common bacteria found in food and left those which are thankfully rare to the end.

- **Salmonella (classified into over 2,000 types)**

Method of infection or poisoning: Poisoning by infection. Living organisms multiply in food and generally large quantities need to be consumed before poisoning occurs.

Source and ideal growth medium: Salmonella is found in animal feedstuffs and organic fertilisers. Organism found in animal excreta, meat products, water polluted with sewage, eggs, poultry, and is also subject to cross infection from animal to animal and human to human. Ideal temperature for growth is 98.6°F. Common mediums raw or undercooked meat, poultry, sausage meat, eggs and pet meat.

Frequency in U.K.: Between the beginning of this year up till mid-March there were 8,000 reported cases. There were 5,000 in the same period last year. This shows that salmonella is still on the increase.

Symptoms and duration: Incubation can vary between six hours and two days after consumption of affected food. The symptoms are fever, headache, aching of limbs and joints, diarrhoea and sometimes vomiting. Duration of illness one to seven days.

Treatment: After diagnosis doctors are reluctant to offer treatment in most cases of food poisoning as diarrhoea tends to expel the organism from the intestine naturally in a fairly short time. The use of Kaolin mixture or similar preparation could prolong the illness. Antibiotics are usually ineffective and may increase the chance of you becoming a carrier. Recommended treatment is bed rest, no food for the duration of diarrhoea but plenty of fluids. If you have persistent or reoccurring symptoms you should visit your doctor.

Method of prevention: Salmonella is killed at temperatures of 55°C (131°F). For safety ensure that meat is cooked to at least that temperature throughout. Wash hands before handling food and in between handling different foods. Keep surfaces and utensils washed between preparing different foods. Keep raw and cooked meat separate. Keep foods refrigerated. Warm foods breed bacteria. If illness occurs cut the risk of spread infection by saving a sample of suspected food for analysis and report the illness to your G.P. for confirmation of the diagnosis of the disease and its type.

● **Campylobacter jejuni**

Method of infection or poisoning: By infection with bacilli in food. It is thought that low doses of campylobacter can cause illness.

Source and ideal growth medium: Found in poultry, meat, milk, water, and on birds and dogs. Grows best in reduced oxygen mediums. Often transmitted in raw or imperfectly pasteurized milk and untreated water. Humans and dogs can be carriers. Cross-contamination can result from careless handling of different meats. They can grow at an optimum temperature of 43°C (109°F).

Frequency in U.K.: 29,000 recorded cases in 1988 and 5,000 cases up to March this year.

Symptoms and duration: Family outbreaks affecting children are common. The incubation is three to five

159

days. The symptoms are stomach cramps followed by strong, revolting smelling stools often stained with yellowish bile and blood. Headaches, fever, dizziness, nausea, but rarely vomiting. Pain often remains after diarrhoea has stopped and relapses are known to occur.

Treatment: Once diagnosis is established, usually no medical treatment is recommended. Bed rest, no foods but plenty of fluids. If the symptoms persist, seek medical advice. You may need the services of a vet as cats and dogs can contract campylobacter from cross-infection. Persistent cases can, and often are, treated when considered medically necessary.

Method of prevention: As we can be carriers, hand washing and personal hygiene will cut down the risks. Ensure that meat and chicken is properly cooked. Also wash hands after stroking pets, especially if there is campylobacter in the household.

● **Listeria monocytogenes**

Method of infection or poisoning: By ingestion of pathogen.

Source and ideal growth medium: Listeria is everywhere, in the soil, animals, surface water and on vegetation. It is resistant to heat and subject to cross-infection. Ideal medium: soft cheeses, cook-chill foods, pre-packed salads and milk. It multiplies at temperatures as low as 0°C.

Frequency in U.K.: 291 reported cases in 1988. Appears to be on the increase.

Symptoms and duration: Incubation is up to 4 weeks. Symptoms range from flu-like illness to meningitis. Infection in pregnant women may lead to still-birth, abortion or severe medical problems for the new-born. Also people with impaired immunity are at risk.

Treatment: Medical advice should be sought to establish a diagnosis. Antibiotic treatment may be prescribed in serious cases.

Method of prevention: At risk people should avoid eating soft cheese, thoroughly re-heat food, follow directions if cooking food in a microwave and always include standing time. Wash all salads carefully and follow eat-by dates.

● **Bacillus cereus**

Method of infection or poisoning: Spores that germinate into bacilli in warm conditions, which then produce a toxin in the food.

Source and ideal growth medium: Present in soil where vegetables, rice and cereals grow. Nicknamed the take-away syndrome, because of the habit of pre-cooking rice in bulk and then leaving it to cool in ambient temperatures. This provides ideal conditions for the toxins to be produced. They are very heat-resistant. They will not be destroyed at temperatures of 120°C if cooked for over an hour. So when the rice is re-cooked the toxins remain. This organism grows best in an oxygen-rich atmosphere.

Frequency in U.K.: Very common.

Symptoms and duration: Symptoms can either be:

1) sudden nausea, vomiting occurring within one to three hours, occasional diarrhoea.
2) acute diarrhoea within nine to 18 hours and occasional vomiting. Recovery should occur within 12 to 24 hours.

Treatment: No medical treatment recommended. Bed rest, no food and plenty of fluids. If symptoms persist seek medical advice.

Method of prevention: Avoid long storage of moist cooked foods. Refrigerate foods rather than cooling at ambient temperatures. Do not add batches of unused rice, vegetables and cereals to new batches of food. Avoid cooking rice in bulk, just cook the required amount and throw away any left over.

● Escherichia coli (includes E. coli gastroenteritis infections)

Method of infection or poisoning: Living bacteria in food causes infection.

Source and ideal growth medium: Food, water and faeces. Always present in faeces, usually enters kitchen in meat, chickens, animal food and by poor personal hygiene practices, i.e. not washing hands after defecation.

Frequency in U.K.: Many cases of this illness probably go unreported, so it may be quite common.

Symptoms and duration: Bacilli often responsible for:
1) Gastro-enteritis in infants, adults and travellers.
2) Illness in older children and adults.

It's divided into four groups: EPEC, ETEC, EIEC, EHEC. Your G.P. will tell you more. Symptoms are: diarrhoea with mucus and blood staining. Incubation is 14 hours to two days. Duration is up to seven days.

Treatment: This type of infection is very serious in babies and medical attention should be sought within 24 hours of onset. Fluid replacement is the most important aspect of treatment. In adults, seek medical attention for correct diagnosis.

Method of prevention: Extreme care to wash hands afer defacation and in dealing with faeces in general, e.g. washing nappies, caring for the sick, and cleaning toilets. Do not let faecal material come into contact with sinks that are used for food preparation.

● **Clostridium perfringens**

Method of infection or poisoning: Another organism that produces spores which remain dormant in food, surviving heat and dehydration. Poisoning is caused by bacilli which produce toxins released in our intestine.

Source and ideal growth medium: Present in excreta of animals and humans. Likely in raw meat, and cold meats. The spores are activated by cooking when they produce the bacilli. No oxygen is needed so pies, casseroles and gravy are ideal mediums for growth. Large concentrations need to be consumed to survive the acid conditions of the stomach.

Frequency in U.K.: Fairly rare. It tends to be associated with social functions.

Symptoms and duration: Incubation is two to 28 hours,

after eating contamined food. The symptoms are stomach ache, violent diarrhoea, nausea but only occasional vomiting. Duration is one to two days.

Treatment: After diagnosis no medical treatment is recommended. Bed rest, no food and plenty of fluids. If symptoms persist seek further medical advice.

Method of prevention: Cool cooked food rapidly before refrigeration. Make up gravy in small quantities and dispose of any left over. Ensure even heating throughout in bulk cooking.

● Staphylococcus aureus

Method of infection or poisoning: Heavy contamination produces poison in foods. The toxins are formed by the organism growing in the food before it is eaten.

Source and ideal growth medium: Humans are the source. The bacteria is found in our skin, noses, throats and in cuts and abrasions. The bug is passed onto cold meats, cream, custards, jellies, and other pre-cooked foods. It is destroyed by heat, but once contamination has occurred, the toxins are resistant to heat and cannot easily be destroyed.

Frequency in U.K.: Not common.

Symptoms and duration: Incubation is between one and six hours. Symptoms are vomiting, stomach ache, sweating, exhaustion, diarrhoea and occasionally collapse. Recovery is usually between six and 24 hours.

Treatment: Once diagnosis is established there is usually no medical treatment recommended. Bed rest, no food and plenty of fluids. If symptoms persist seek further medical advice.

Method of prevention: Avoid touching nose or mouth, sneezing over food during preparation. Make sure you cover any infected wound with water-tight plaster. Store at risk foods for a minimum amount of time in cold storage and be careful if you have a boil, stye or carbuncle as they also could be infected with staphylococcus.

● **Yersinia enterocolitica**

Method of infection or poisoning: An animal pathogen affecting man.

Source and ideal growth medium: Pets and animals are the usual source of infection. Organisms can be found in dairy products, both raw and pasteurized milk, cream, ice cream and many meat products. This organism can grow on foods stored in the refrigerator.

Frequency in U.K.: Not a common cause of enteritis.

Symptoms and duration: Incubation is between 24 and 36 hours. Symptoms are abdominal cramps, fever, diarrhoea and vomiting. Duration is three to five days. In severe cases relapses may occur up to eight months after the first illness. Since it is found in some dairy products, children are often the victims of this illness.

Treatment: Usually no medical treatment is recommended. Bed rest, no food and plenty of fluids. Do seek medical advice to establish a correct diagnosis and if you suffer from relapses.

Method of prevention: Careful refrigerator management. Throw away foods beyond their eat by date.

● Streptococcus (over 80 serological types)

Method of infection or poisoning: By infection and possibly toxins formed in foods. Many microbiologists feel that little is known about this organism and what is known is confusing.

Source and ideal growth medium: Foods suspected of carrying streptococcus are raw milk, custard, ham, and egg salads. Organism passed to these mediums by contact of hands, nose or saliva.

Frequency in U.K.: This is rare and needs specific diagnosis.

Symptoms and duration: Symptoms are septic sore throat, and sometimes stomach aches, sickness and diarrhoea. There are different types of streptococcus and other symptoms may include upper respiratory tract infections including pneumonia. Incubation is between three and 22 hours. Duration is between one and two days in less serious cases.

Treatment: Diagnosis can be confirmed after throat swab tests by your G.P.

Method of prevention: Do not allow hands to come into contact with nose or saliva whilst preparing foodstuffs. Do not smoke whilst preparing food as fingers can come into contact with saliva and food.

• Vibrio parahaemolyticus

Method of infection or poisoning: A marine organism passed on by consuming raw or cooked fish from polluted waters. Infection caused by bacillus called a vibrio.

Source and ideal growth medium: Found in sea foods especially raw fish. Cross-contamination possible from cooked to un-cooked fish. The bacillus needs oxygen to grow. More common in the Far East but outbreaks have occurred in this country.

Frequency in U.K.: Very rare.

Symptoms and duration: Incubation is between 14 and 15 hours. Symptoms may develop rapidly with chronic diarrhoea and subsequent dehydration. Vomiting and fever are not uncommon. Stomach cramps may last two to five days. The illness resembles a mild form of cholera.

Treatment: Usually no medical treatment is recommended. Bed rest, no food and plenty of fluids. You should consult your doctor initially to obtain a correct diagnosis and also if symptoms persist.

Method of prevention: Buy good quality prawns and crab meat especially if they are imported. Take care when handling cooked and uncooked fish to avoid cross-infection.

• Clostridium botulinum

Method of infection or poisoning: The organism grows a powerful toxin that affects the nervous system. Unlike most bacterial toxins, they are pre-formed in the food and already poisonous when taken by mouth. Fatal in 50% of cases. Organism destroyed by cooking.

Source and ideal growth medium: Common inhabitant of soil, in spores, from where it contaminates foodstuffs that provide anaerobic conditions (without oxygen). It appears in preserved foods, particularly canned foods. There is litle risk from commercially canned foods but home canning of meats and home bottling of vegetables with low acidity levels are the greatest danger.

Frequency in U.K.: Very rare.

Symptoms and duration: Incubation period is approximately 18 to 36 hours. Symptoms are fatigue, headaches, dilation of pupils, dizziness, initial diarrhoea followed by acute constipation. There is disturbance of speech and vision. Often the respiratory centres become paralysed leading to death. Those who survive will need a long convalescence.

Treatment: With immediate medical attention and if diagnosed early, the outcome is less likely to be fatal. If an anti-toxin is given within hours of eating the affected food the outcome is likely to be favourable.

Method of prevention: Avoid eating home canned foods and home bottled vegetables. Also avoid eating meat products from damaged cans.

Emergency stations

It is also worth emphasising again the difference between food which is itself poisonous due to the presence of harmful bugs or toxins and food which merely acts as a carrier for the bacteria which once in your gut become harmful. The doctors and scientists distinguished the two by talking about food poisoning and food borne infections.

Food poisoning – bacillus cereus, clostridium perfringes, staphylococcus aureus, clostridium botulinum.

Food borne infections – salmonella, campylobacter jejeuni, listeria monocytogenes, escherichia coli, yersinia enterocolitica, vibrio parahaemolyticus.

Surprisingly, the recent growth in food related illness is almost completely linked not to food poisoning but to food borne infections. In other words we have created the conditions in which harmful bacteria can flourish in our food. The positive side of this is we can take steps to prevent the bugs multiplying and we have tried to give you some advice on how to do this. However, this means the consumer is effectively the equivalent of a fire fighter coping with an emergency – we would like to see more steps being taken as we have indicated earlier to prevent the food becoming a home for harmful bacteria in the first place.

POSTCRIPT:
1992 AND ALL THAT

For most of the book we have concentrated on looking at how our government, farmers, water suppliers and food manufacturers could respond to the problems here at home. We have also looked at what we as consumers can do to help ourselves. In this chapter we take a look at some of the issues raised by 1992 – the date by which all trade barriers between European community countries are due to come down.

Last year we imported nearly nine billion pounds worth of food, the majority of which came from our European partners. As the trade barriers are removed, will we be faced with a flood of food imports from Europe? Will those infamous butter mountains and wine lakes end up on British tables? Will we be at risk from lower hygiene standards which some people claim are tolerated in some European countries? Will the new rules on food inspection be adequate? Will our livestock be threatened by disease as some British vets have argued? As consumers we need to try and find out what will be done in these areas in order to avoid a fresh crop of problems arising in the 1990's.

EEC versus national standards

At the time of writing (April 1989) it is still far from clear where the dividing line between EEC regulations and national ones will be drawn. Take for example the issue of what is called composition or recipe law. Some European countries have in the past tried to maintain food standards by defining the composition of their food. For example, until recently the Germans would not admit into their country anyone else's sausages or beer unless they conformed to the Federal Republic's idea of what constituted a proper banger or a decent pint. Similarly German pasta products which often contain soft wheat were until recently not allowed into France and Italy. German apple vinegar raised objections in Italy where it was thought that vinegar should only be made from wine. The Dutch have been uneasy about Germany boiling sausages because they contained the additive lactoprotein. The French remain adamant about what should be in frozen yoghurt and Edam (yes, Edam) cheese.

Where does the European Commission stand in this great debate? Initially it spent its time trying to break down barriers to trade. One of the key judgements dates back to 1979 and was given in what is known as the Cassis de Dijon case. It concerned a French trader who had been unsuccessfully trying to export red currant flavoured aperitif, Cassis de Dijon, into West Germany. The European Court of Justice in its ruling developed what is referred to as 'the mutual recognition principles'. These state that a product legally manufactured and marketed in one member state of the EEC must automatically be allowed to be sold in another EEC country, provided it is *safe* and provided it is *properly* and *adequately labelled*.

While this judgement may seem eminently sensible, many Europeans were far from happy with it. If national standards in one country are low they argue, then these inferior standards will simply be spread across the community. Tim Stocker of the Food and Drink Federation disagrees with these critics. He argues that: 'the quality of the kind under discussions – ie not microbiological quality but the composition of the product – is subjective. Consumers make choices from a range of safe and wholesome products on offer. Claims about quality are made by those who wish to preserve the status quo in order to protect agriculture or a sector of industry which could not stand up to competition.'

Although it may be true that some opposition has come from those people indicated by Tim Stocker, there has also been opposition from consumer groups. These groups see the prospect of hard won standards being allowed to slip in order to worship at the altar of free competition.

But what about the area where *common* EEC standards rule OK? We have already seen earlier in this book that the EEC has set rules on additives, drinking water, hormone usage and is considering flavourings. In what other areas can we expect the EEC to impose rules which all European member states must follow? With the the approach of 1992 the EEC decided it must adopt a more positive stance than the policy outlined and implicit in the mutual recognition principles. In its 1985 white paper it stated that common EEC standards are only required to protect public health, provide consumers with adequate information, ensure fair trading and to provide certain controls of food production and marketing. Some four years later the EEC is still working on its draft hygiene rules which were due to be unveiled in Spring 1989 but have yet to see the light of day.

Is this new approach satisfactory? Will the outcome not depend on the political clout of certain members within the EEC? Will the need to reach an acceptable consensus lead to a watering down of standards? All these questions are impossible to answer at this stage. However, recent history produces a mixed verdict on the EEC food regulations. For example in 1987 we abandoned our national standard which stated that certain meat products must contain a minimum quantity of meat and replaced it with an EEC ruling that the percentage of meat included should be stated. The result was a decline in the average minimum amount of meat in so-called 'meat' products. True we as consumers knew for the first time exactly how much meat was in our meat products, but standards dropped. The fear is that this example will be repeated over and over again and that economic pressures will drive down food standards to the lowest common denominator in the EEC. This would then lead to a situation where only those who can afford to pay higher prices will be able to enjoy the quality of food they have come to expect.

The problem is similar to that of throwing the baby out with the bath water. Should we abandon all national standards simply because some of these standards may be anti fair trading? We agree with the Consumers in the European Community Group who argue that a case by case approach is needed based on a detailed study of each country's existing rules. The aim should be to ensure minimum quality of basic foodstuffs while at the same time removing the shackles on the food industry. A delicate balancing act is required but some composition standards are needed if people are to be confident that when they buy for example meat products, they know they are buying a product largely made of meat. Adequate labelling is no replacement for basic standards, rather it is an additional aid to choice.

As 1992 edges nearer, more and more decisions about the regulations covering the food we eat are likely to be taken by the European commission. Once again the message from the recent past is far from reassuring. The case of the EEC ban on the use of growth promoters for beef cattle is an interesting example. At the beginning of 1987 following a spate of distressing stories about small Italian children with enlarged genitals the EEC outlawed the use of all beef hormones. The ban included five hormones which virtually all the world experts have now concluded are safe and have no harmful side effects. Has this blanket ban really protected the consumer? A black market in stronger, more dangerous hormone cocktails has developed in countries such as Belgium and West Germany (if not all over the community) and we may well be eating imported meat from animals treated with these dangerous hormones. A review of the hormone ban is underway and urgent action is required.

The issue of irradiation which we have already touched upon in chapter three is likely to split the community. The use of irradiation, except in carefully controlled hospital environments was banned in the UK at the time of writing but in other countries such as the Netherlands it is permitted. Under the Cassis de Dijon ruling a Dutch company could go to the European court and argue that irradiated food be accepted in the UK since scientists at both the EEC and in the international community could be called as witnesses to say it was safe. The EEC in order to avoid this has stated that this is an area where *common* EEC standards, not national ones, must be upheld.

The trouble is what should these common standards be? At present the EEC proposal – which will not become law until it is agreed by the member states and the European parliament – is that irradiation should be permitted subject to strict regulations. These include maximum limits on the overall dosages of radiation for certain specific categories of food which are more strict than those advocated by the World Health Organisation, rules on the plants where radiation techniques would be carried out but no requirement for food to be labelled. Consumer pressure may well result in the proposals being amended to include labelling but since at present we cannot detect when food has been irradiated, it is difficult to see how this rule could be policed. As this book went to press is looked likely that the UK government would jump the EEC starting gun and introduce irradiation, although it was not clear whether or not it would adopt the suggested regulations outlined in the EEC's proposal.

EEC labelling

We have already come across some of the issues about adequate labelling in the chapter on chemicals in our food and throughout this book we have emphasised the importance of labelling as an *additional* means of ensuring the safety and quality of our food. The EEC

for the consumer is that the whole process is and lengthy that valuable time is being the very real worry at the end of the be imposed that as a result of

has in several instances provided us with a lead on this matter. For example, the UK 'sell-by' date which we have criticised will not be permitted after 1992 when it will have to be replaced by a 'best before' date for most foods and a 'use by' date for highly perishable foods. Long life, including canned foods, and frozen foods will also have to be datemarked.

The EEC is also considering tougher measures on the labelling of food for special nutritional categories such as slimmers, sportsmen etc. This will cover claims about fat and sugar content as well as other matters including vitamins, calories and minerals. Such measures are long overdue, especially as there is a growing and highly competitive market in these products and it is an area where the consumer can easily be mislead by a welter of claims and counter-claims.

Preparation and distribution

Up till now much of the EEC's regulations on food has been devoted to the thorny issues of standards and labelling, but there are signs the new battle ground will be the preparation and distribution of food. This whole area is very important as we can expect a growing intra-community trade in food and as the issue of contamination along the food chain, which we have discussed in detail in this book, gains in prominence. It is worth emphasising yet again at this point that even if irradiation is introduced this does not stop the food becoming contaminated after it has left the factory.

There are two key issues here:
− setting high common standards for food preparation and distribution.

– ensuring that these high standards are followed.

It is too early to make any judgements on the standards the EEC plans to set in this crucial area since its draft directive is not available. So far it has announced plans to tighten up measures aimed at preventing packaging or other materials migrating into food during preparation, processing or distribution. Specific community legislation already covers cellulose film, ceramic crockery and certain matters concerning plastics. Further directives based on the advice of the commission's scientific committees will focus on plastics, rubber, paper, metals and wood. These piecemeal directives only tackle a small number of outstanding issues and the real test will be the hygiene laws. Britain is not alone in the EEC in having a food industry where national legislation is in many instances outdated and inadequate.

On the question of ensuring that future EEC standards will be met, there must remain a major question mark. There is an old adage, 'where there's a will, there's a way'. Will there be the political will? Will the politicians have the strength to impose the rules on industry, even if this means some of their domestic companies going bust?

It is far too early to answer these questions. What we can say is that according to preliminary investigations by Brussels the quality and quantity of inspection measures differ markedly between member states at present. For instance, in some countries national inspectors are not allowed to make checks at the place of manufacture, i.e. inside the factory. While meaningful comparisons are fraught with difficulties no one in Europe denies that our record is one of the best in the EEC. Food inspectors in Britain must have a degree; their counterparts in Portugal can start on the job with just five weeks' experience.

Many like Caroline Jackson, one of the best informed members of the Strasbourg assembly when it comes to food issues, believes that Brussels must try to harmonise training and qualification norms if consumer confidence is to be maintained. Another problem the EEC has not yet tackled is to how to meet the demands for a Community inspectorate to make sure that any harmonised national rules finally agreed by member states are properly observed.

Trade in live animals

As we have already seen in chapter three, the British Veterinary Association has raised doubts about the import of EEC animals from certain member states where diseases which have been eradicated from Britain still remain prevalent. The danger here is that disease free herds in this country may become infected as much as the direct danger to us, the consumers.

When border posts are dismantled in 1992 checks aimed at avoiding the spread of serious diseases will no longer be made at the frontiers. Instead they must be carried out at the source of production within the member state. This means, for example, that we in Britain will have to rely on the veterinary services and meat inspectors operating in the other member states to protect us. Yet as we have seen these may not be of equally high standard through the community. In addition, to help ease these potential problems the EEC has developed a programme of total eradication of certain diseases so that standards in say Spain and Portugal can be brought up to those elsewhere in the community. States which comply with these standards will officially be designated by Brussels as disease free. The commission has also tabled (but not yet agreed) measures to stop the introduction of exotic diseases from outside the community, to provide on the spot checks of meat premises by commission experts, to ensure that qualified veterinarians supervise and inspect cutting premises for poultry.

Meat and dairy regulations

The commission is also working on detailed hygiene rules for the meat sector but as the recent food scare here shows, common and high standards of hygiene need to be implemented across the food processing sector. The Brussels authorities are currently working on a proposal which pre-dates the listeria and salmonella rows but which is likely to be aimed mainly at the dairy sector. These proposals are slow to develop and even slower to implement since the commission needs to analyse the position in each member state, draw up rules which cover the needs throughout the community and then convince each of the members of the requirement for tougher regulation even if such rules impose harsher burdens on those less developed countries in the EEC where standards are most in need of uprating but where perhaps the economic burden of improvement will be most severe.

The fear for the consumer is that the whole process is so drawn out and lengthy that valuable time is being lost. There is also the very real worry at the end of the day that rules will be imposed that as a result of

political bargaining are insufficiently tough to maintain high standards and protect us from the growth in intra community food trade after 1992. It would be a terrible shame if after improving our own domestic standards of food production, distribution and sale we were to be swamped by inferior food from abroad. It will be up to us, the consumer, to put pressure both on MPs in Westminser and MEPs in Strasbourg to ensure that 1992 does not produce more problems than it solves as far as the food industry is concerned.

Acknowledgements

This book could not have been written without the generous help of a large number of people who shared their expertise and time with us. They did so in the belief that you, the consumer, have the right to be informed about important issues relating to your health and the way the food industry is run. We would also like to thank Tim Dickson, the *Financial Times* correspondent in Brussels, for agreeing to contribute the chapter on Europe.

While it would take another book to thank personally all those who helped us, we would like to say a special thank you to the following people:

Mr Roger Armstrong
Chairman of the Food and Education Group at the Institute of Environmental Health Officers.

Professor David Conning
Director-General, British Nutrition Foundation.

Dr. Paul Gibbs
Leatherhead Food Research Association.

Amanda and Matthew Jupp
Listeriosis sufferers.

Mr. Ian McFadyen, FRCOG
Department of Obstetrics and Gynaecology at the Royal Liverpool Hospital.

Mr. Frederick Osbourne
Principal Environmental Health Officer from Northampton Borough Council.

Dr. John Parks
Department of Microbiology at Reading University.

Dr. L. W. Poulter
Senior Lecturer in Inflammatory Disease Research, Department of Immunology at the Royal Free Hospital School of Medicine.

Mr. Bill Reilly
British Veterinary Association.

Thames Water Authority
For their case history.

Laura Thomas
Campaign for the Freedom of Information.

Dr. Verner Wheelock
Leader of the Food Policy Research Unit at Bradford University.

In addition, a number of organisations helped considerably. These included: Consumers in the European Community Group, Department of Environment, Department of Health, Foresight, Hillsdown Holdings, Marks and Spencer Plc, Ministry for Agriculture, Fisheries and Food, NALGO, National Farmers' Union, Scottish Office and the Water Research Centre.

Further reading

Communicable Diseases by Wilfrid H. Parry, published by Hodder and Stoughton. ISBN 0-340-24291-4.

Consumer Law in the EEC by Geoffrey Woodroffe, published by Sweet and Maxwell, London. ISBN 0-421-32640-9.

Food Adulteration and How To Beat It. London Food Commission, published by Unwin. ISBN 0-04-440212-0.

Food Fit To Eat. British Nutrition Foundation. Sphere Books. ISBN 0-7474-0314-7.

Food Poisoning and Food Hygiene (5th Edition) by Betty C. Hobbs and Diane Roberts, published by Edward Arnold. ISBN 0-7131-4516-1.

Immunity Plus by Arabella Melville and Colin Johnson, published by Penguin Books. ISBN 0-1400-9392-3.

Medical Microbiology (5th Edition) by C. G. A. Thomas, published by Bailliere Tindall. ISBN 0-7020-0997-0.

Prodfact 1988 by Daphne MacCarthy. British Food Information Service. 1989 edition in process of compilation.

The Food Labelling Regulations 1984. HMSO No. 1305. ISBN 0-11-047305-1.

The Prevention of Pollution by R. M. E. Diamant, published by Pitman Publishing. ISBN 0-273-31819-5.

The Residues Report by Stephanie Lashford, published by Thorsons. ISBN 0-7225-1481-6.

Viruses, Allergies and the Immune System by Jan De Vries, published by Mainstream Publishing. ISBN 1-85158-176-6.

ALSO AVAILABLE FROM ROSTERS

TALKING TURKEY by Alison Rice (£5.95)

A lively and entertaining look at this newest holiday sensation. Travel writer and broadcaster Alison Rice has produced an up-to-date guide to the main Turkish resorts and Istanbul. Aimed at visitors new to Turkey it explains what to see, where to stay — and equally important, what to avoid. Includes basic Turkish phrases plus hints on making the best of the food, wine and shopping available.

VIVA ESPANA by Edmund Swinglehurst (£5.95)

Discover the real Spain before the bulldozers and industrialists have destroyed its natural beauty. In this comprehensive guide to Spain, Edmund Swinglehurst, travel expert and author, has provided a fascinating glimpse behind the veil of Spain to show you the heart of the countryside, its people, its culture and its way of life.

CHAMPAGNE ON A BUDGET by Patrick Delaforce (£5.95)

Champagne is probably the world's most famous wine — yet few people have discovered the sparkling region where it is produced. Wine expert and travel writer Patrick Delaforce shows you how to enjoy a trip to the Champagne region, suggests tours, visits to vineyards and gives advice on the wines worth sampling. Aimed at the independent traveller who does not wish to bust his budget this book includes lists of medium priced hotels and restaurants plus handy hints on enjoying your stay.

FRENCH RIVIERA ON A BUDGET by Patrick Delaforce (£5.95)

The land of celebrities, champagne cocktails and caviare is just waiting to be discovered. In this timely guide travel writer Patrick Delaforce shows that you don't need to break the Bank at Monte Carlo to enjoy a stay among the rich and famous along the world's famous Cote d'Azur. He lists medium priced hotels, restaurants plus plenty of advice on how to spend those sun filled days and fun filled nights.

BURGUNDY AND BEAUJOLAIS ON A BUDGET by Patrick Delaforce (£5.95)

Discover one of France's most beautiful wine regions without spending a fortune. Patrick Delaforce, wine expert and travel writer, reveals the true heart of the French countryside. Just one hour's drive from Paris lies Burgundy, famous the world over for its wines, but also one of the most beautiful and intriguing regions in France. For the gourmet there is the chance to visit the vineyards where Chablis and Beaujolais are made and sample local produce such as truffles, river fish, fine game and fresh fruits. Includes: regional tours, local wines and wine co-operatives, value for money accommodation and restaurants, places of interest, regional events.

GASCONY AND ARMAGNAC ON A BUDGET by Patrick Delaforce (£5.95)

Discover one of France's best kept secrets — the land of brandy, beaches and Basque cuisine. Wine expert and travel writer Patrick Delaforce reveals the heart of one of France's most inviting holiday locations. From the beautiful silver coast fringed with pine forests through to the inland villages, there is an alluring countryside just waiting to be discovered. Magnificent beaches, sophisticated nightlife and superb cuisine. Includes: regional tours, local wines and wine co-operatives, value for money hotels and restaurants, places of interest and regional events.

IS IT WORTH ANYTHING? by Stephen Ellis (£3.99)

Most of us have drawers filled with odds and ends. But are they worth anything? Stephen Ellis writes on the money pages of the Daily Mirror which gets thousands of letters from readers asking just that. So here for everyone who cannot bear to throw anything away 'just in case' is the book which will give most of the answers. Includes: toys, stamps, glass, jewellery, postcards, records and much more.

COOK AND HOUSEWIFE'S MANUAL by Mistress Margaret Dods (hardback £14.95)

With an introduction by Glynn Christian

Discover the world of Mistress Margaret Dods and the Cleikum Club. Mistress Dods was the founder of one of the first cookery clubs in the country and her manual, first published in 1829, includes the story of how the club was set up, over 1,000 recipes as well as hints on wine making, curing meats and making cheese. Glynn Christian says 'It is a real cookery book, a book for people who really like to eat. Comic and revelatory'. Recommended by Chat and the Glasgow Herald.

NEW FEMALE INSTRUCTOR (hardback £12.50)

First published in the 1830's the book was designed to be a practical manual aimed at turning every one of its fair readers into an intelligent and pleasing companion. It includes: dress, fashion, morals, love, courtship, duties of the married state, conduct to servants plus more than 100 pages of recipes. Lively, entertaining — the perfect gift.

THE SHARE BOOK (3rd ed) by Rosemary Burr (£5.99)

With an introduction by the Rt. Hon. Mrs. Margaret Thatcher

An up-to-date, completely revised edition of this bestselling guide to the stockmarket which has been bought by more than 50,000 people. Includes advice on every aspect of buying, selling and choosing shares. A full glossary, details of members of the Stock Exchange, Unit Trust Association and Association of Investment Trust Companies. Plus new rules on investor protection and unit trust pricing. The classic companion for anyone interested in stocks and shares.

YOUR BUSINESS IN 1992 by James Dewhurst (£6.95)

Chartered accountant, author and authority on business management, James Dewhurst has distilled his experience into this valuable addition to any businessman's library. What will the much heralded internal market in Europe mean in pratice to you and your business? The answers are inside. Includes: setting common standards, enforcing technical requirements, competing for orders from public bodies, distribution services, prospects for take-overs and mergers, new tax environment and much more.

HOMEOWNERS SURVIVAL GUIDE ed. Rosemary Burr (£3.95)

Recommended by the Financial Times, the Sun and the Times. Everything the homeowner needs to make the most of his or her investment and run their home cost effectively. Includes: choosing your home, arranging the finance, count-down to purchase, insurance, decoration, home improvement moving on and cost cutting ideas.